WALES
Nation and Region

WALES
NATION and REGION

Mervyn Phillips

First Impression—1997

ISBN 1 85902 423 8

© Mervyn Phillips

Mervyn Phillips has asserted his right under the Copyright,
Designs and Patents Act, 1988, to be identified as Author of this Work.

Printed in Wales at
Gomer Press, Llandysul, Ceredigion

CONTENTS

PREFACE

This book is based on a series of lectures given for the Workers Education Association in Wrexham and I am grateful to them and to the group that came to the lectures for their interest and support. As will quickly be seen, this is a general survey of Wales as a nation and region and I have relied on well known authorities for my main sources, particularly when dealing with historical issues. There is a bibliography at the end of each chapter and I have tried to indicate in the text where there is a direct quote. The importance of some authors will be obvious. My thanks to them and to all who have helped put materials together and given assistance in preparing the script.

M.H.P.

Chapter 1

INTRODUCTION

In 1991 a delegation from Clwyd visited Czechoslovakia to promote economic and cultural links. It met President Miklosko of the Slovakian Assembly who was interested in Wales's status as a nation and wanted to know how it was that a country could have a national team playing in the European cup but not even have a regional assembly. To a Czechoslovakian, as he was at the time, there appeared to be something to be explained about a country which was seen as one of Europe's oldest communities and yet had no democratic institutions.

The issues of nationality and regions were particularly important in Czechoslovakia's new-found freedom from communism. The President said that when Mrs Thatcher had visited Bratislava, the capital of Slovakia, he had asked her about regions in Britain and especially whether there were any problems in Scotland and Wales, but was told that there were no constitutional issues in the regions in Britain. Mr Miklosko should not have been surprised, because over the previous sixty years, since the time of the great economic depression, there had been a consensus in the Labour and Conservative Parties that shared this view—the Welsh Labour leader Aneurin Bevan was one to state it firmly in Parliament and elsewhere. We were able to explain to our host that a change had taken place in Britain and that constitutional proposals for Scotland and Wales were before the country because the Labour Party had declared a firm commitment to a Parliament for Scotland and an Assembly for Wales if elected to government. Among the other parties in Wales, both Plaid Cymru and the Liberal Democrats would be pressing for a commitment to devolution to be met speedily and the Conservative Party, while still unwilling to accept the case for a regional assembly to improve accountability of government, was pressing on with the growth of regional powers.

Since those discussions in 1991, some of the regions of the former Communist block, as in the case of Slovakia, have opted for separation but such a course was not inevitable and, on the contrary, in many cases Central and Eastern Europeans have found a place for their regions within a united country. Similarly in the UK, the argument in support of the Union is not at all at odds with the proposals for democratic accountability at the regional level. Indeed, supporters of some form of devolution suggest that Westminster might be strengthened by being able to concentrate on the central issues of government.

THE UNITED KINGDOM—A MULTI-NATIONAL STATE

The background to any constitutional reform in Wales involves the relationship between Britain as a whole and its different parts and needs some answers to questions about the nature of the nation and the state. Britain has been described as a multinational state made up of England, Scotland, Wales and Northern Ireland; one state and several nations. Whether or not people in Wales, or in the other nations of the UK, feel a strong sense of separate nationality, we are British subjects. We belong to a state—the United Kingdom—that seems to meet the traditional test of a sovereign political unit which is that it should be constitutionally self contained and have sovereignty within its boundaries. It is, apparently, not subject to any outside power and the people are constitutionally considered the subjects of the realm, required to obey the law and at the same time are protected by it. This is what you would expect in a centralised state which does not share powers with either the nations or regions within it. Changes are, however, taking place because of the role of Europe, and the traditional position would be affected, too, if devolution came.

The unity of the UK did not come about all at once. If the Acts of Union are taken as the dates of union with England—Wales (1536 and 1542), Scotland (1707) and Ireland (1800), N. Ireland since 1922; it may be taken that those are the dates when legally allegiance was made to the Crown, whether to the monarch personally or the Crown in parliament, and that the right to protection of the subjects by the state has followed.

As will be seen the claim to sovereignty over Wales was made by the English king well before 1536 but, as there was a view that the Tudor kings were Welsh, it is suggested that the Acts in 1536 and 1542, reflect the earliest legitimation of the Union.

Apart from the constitutional aspects of a Union of the nations, there is always the possibility that over the years the dominant partner will culturally and economically assimilate the other nation and, in the case of Wales, it seemed likely for more than 200 years after the Act of Union that Wales would become part of greater England subject to the English Crown, English Law and the Church of England.

Signs of the cultural assimilation remain: there are still times when people outside Wales refer to Welsh towns as being in England and to Welsh people as being English. Even some Welsh people may remember singing 'There'll always be an England' and identifying with the song. Change has, however, taken place here as well and the process stopped—this may be illustrated by the practice of the Wrexham Lager Co which in the 1900s had an excellent advertising poster but with the Brewery address given as Wrexham, North Wales, England. Recently the company have matched the present mood by producing their lager cans bilingually. This move, small in itself, reflects the growing consciousness among Welsh people of being Welsh, as well as British.

National pride, affection and identity, whether British or Welsh, is important as a natural bonding of peoples and should not be dismissed. There is, of course, a danger of it being perverted, so it is as well to acknowledge that danger and be aware that national pride can lead to an arrogance which overestimates the value of one's own nation and wrongly despises others. Archbishop Carey, speaking to the European Parliament in 1993, distinguished between national identity and nationalism and emphasised that it is the latter which is the danger. He said, 'Nationalism will not tolerate a multilayered sense of identity and seeks to take over other layers or eliminate them.' Whether the Archbishop's identification of nationalism as the perverted form of nationality identity is correct, the sentiments behind his speech are in line with the present argument.

Territorial areas like Wales—without a coterminous state—are obviously stateless, but if not assimilated within the larger whole may keep their sense of nationality and community. In Wales the culture, especially the language, has been important in keeping the Welsh identity. The language was described by Saunders Lewis, first president of Plaid Cymru (the Welsh Nationalist Party), as the ancestral home for the nation and initially Plaid Cymru argued a case

11

for political independence in order to protect the Welsh language. More recently, however, they have dropped this view in favour of the concept of community and belonging as the basis of nationality. It is seen that the language is linked to the nation but is now only one factor sustaining Welsh nationality. In any case, for almost all of this century English, in the form spoken in Wales, has been the majority monoglot language of people in Wales, and the Welsh language (Cymraeg) has become a minority language spoken by some 20% of the population of Wales. The culture of the community is more than the language and is often not dependent upon it at all. As a former Labour secretary of state (George Thomas) has said, some of the most Welsh places in Wales are not Welsh-speaking at all.

If community rather than the language is seen as the bond for the Welsh nation, it is easier to recognise language as both a factor in making that bond and as the basis for a separate minority culture in Wales. In a UK setting there are at least two minority cultures in Wales—the Welsh culture based on Cymraeg and the Welsh culture which is based upon the English language (in much the same way as American culture is based upon English). John Osmond suggests there are, in fact, three cultural groups in Wales—Y Fro Gymraeg (Welsh-speaking Wales), Valleys Wales (which is mainly English speaking but strongly Welsh in outlook) and British Wales (which again is mainly English speaking and considers itself as English in Wales); and Dai Smith in *Wales! Wales?* quotes from Sir Alfred Zimmerman in a similar threefold grouping—Welsh Wales, industrial or working class Wales and English or upper class Wales.

Whether there are two or three, or more, cultural groups in Wales, it is only in sharing in the community of Wales as a whole, with a common sense of belonging, that it is possible to speak of an increased sense of Welsh identity. It may be that the change among the Welsh towards its own consciousness is because more people understand that speaking Cymraeg is not the test of being Welsh and each of the cultural groups can form part of the heritage of Wales and as such deserves support from the whole of Wales.

A community of interest which creates a nation can be based on a shared culture, education, social and economic experience or a combination of these. It need have little to do with present sovereignty and statehood and what is important is how people regard themselves and their community. Poets write about it in English and in Welsh— 'not the contours but the people who live there and have lived there' is how Dannie Abse approaches nationality. 'What is being a nation?' asked Waldo Williams in Welsh and 'A talent springing from the heart' was the reply. (*'Beth yw bod yn genedl? Dawn yn nwfa y galon.'*) It expresses a present belief in belonging to a community which is a nation with its particular and defined history.

The past is still important because it relates the people to the country through the sense of belonging to its history. W.E. Gladstone, speaking at the Eisteddfod in Mold in 1873 referred to the 'ancient history, ancient deeds and the ancient language of the principality', (quoted by K. O. Morgan, former Principal of University of Wales, Aberystwyth) and a feeling of continuity is generally part of being at one with a community. It is possible to move from this to such a backward looking view that Wales is considered as a nation which existed only in the past—perhaps when Cymraeg was the dominant language or even when the Welsh had some claim to sovereignty of their own. The poet R.S. Thomas expresses his view: 'There is no present in Wales and no future. There is only the past', and historian Professor Gwyn A. Williams called his TV programme and book *When was Wales?* as though feeling that it was all over for Wales as a nation.

The concern for the past is understandable and the history of Wales is, like that of any country, precious to it and its writers. But to suggest that Wales exists today only as an administrative unit would be wrong. This would ignore the history of Wales, the perceptions of the Welsh people and the changes taking place in Europe which recognise the historic, but stateless, nation as existing alongside the nation state. Some elements of national identity and common culture which are to be found in Wales in the present century together with the formation of its boundary and the historic foundations of nationhood are looked at in Chapter 2.

The changes in attitudes in Wales which have brought a renewed sense of Welshness do not appear to have weakened the sense of being British, rather the reverse. A Mori opinion poll in 1996, published by the *Western Mail*, showed that only twenty per cent thought they were Welsh but not British. If the Welsh people want to be British as well as Welsh it is partly because this makes clear that Welsh people are not English, but it is mainly because of a continuing commitment to the Union which is the United Kingdom. Such identification has little to do with the duties of being a British subject within a sovereign state. It is the sense of being part of a community which is constituted by Britain. While we may be called British subjects, the sense of Britishness arises from belonging to Britain as the homeland rather than as sovereign state. This fits in with a modern view of the state which is that of 'a community coming together for the purposes of government' (Madgwick and Rowe), and might be considered as a replacement of the older concept of the state as sovereign. It may well even be time for notions of sovereignty to be changed, replaced and related to contemporary needs in a move to a community basis.

In Britain there is a particularly strong sense of nationality. Our 'island home' gives a corporate sense of belonging that is not diminished by being Welsh or becoming European. Historian Victor Bogdanor considers that this strong sense of nationality comes from our history, particularly from times of war when the patriotic appeal of the country was to stand up for liberty against the oppressor, whether he was Bonaparte or Hitler or anyone else. It is a bonding of loyalty through history and it is not exclusive to those whose families have lived in Britain for many generations. It includes newer ethnic groups within the nation and, in some cases, the newcomers are even more enthusiastically British than the majority.

The sense of British community is so strong that it is not really adequate to describe Britain as the state which encompasses England, Wales, Scotland and Northern Ireland as the nations of the Union. It is more proper to refer to Britain as being made up of five rather than four nations, with Britain as the nation state, and the four other nations being the kingdoms of England and Scotland, the Principality of Wales and the Province of Northern Ireland making up the Union which forms our nation state. If, as suggested, the nature of the state is of a community coming together for the purposes of government, then it is possible to belong to the nation state and a smaller community

14

like Wales without compromising loyalty to either of them. The same applies to the sense of belonging to a larger community than the nation state, like the European Union, and there is a logic in the UK sharing sovereignty with both the larger unit of Europe and a smaller community like Wales, as they come together for the purposes of government. In Chapter 3 there is further consideration of some issues about sovereignty. After looking at the way sovereignty affected Wales historically, there is a brief review of the concept within the UK and some of the reasons why, until recently at least, it has been difficult to accept devolution or any idea of power-sharing with Westminster.

WALES AS A REGION

One of the reasons given for the renewed sense of identity is that Wales is now seen as a region in the UK and Europe and the significance of these changes in Europe is developed in Chapter 4. One senior EU official, Aneurin Rhys Hughes, wanted to deny that Wales is a region in Europe and said that it takes its place in Europe as a small nation alongside the regions but not as one of them. He suggested that the Maastricht creation of a Committee of the Regions should become a 'Senate of the Regions and Small Nations'. But whatever the particular description adopted, the present position is that Wales shares with Catalonia, Baden Würtemberg, the North West of England and the other regions of Europe the fact of being a region. It is a defined political unit of administration for which the European Union have prepared their map of the regions and included Wales as a region, and this map itself is based upon the UK government's own creation of regions throughout the country.

It is, as will be suggested in Chapters 4 and 5, in the development of the modern administrative unit as a region of government in the UK and Europe that Wales has become politically important in the latter half of the twentieth century. In the UK there has been a three stage development of the region in government. As the welfare state and national economic planning developed, the following were the steps to the establishment of the region as administrative unit: deconcentration, decentralisation and devolution (as identified by Hogwood and Keating in their *Regional Government in England*.) Deconcentration took place when central government could no longer be run solely from the offices of Whitehall and local offices were required, but still with the decision-making in the departmental headquarters in London. Decentralisation followed, when the Government Department concerned passed a range of decisions to regional offices, but still organised them on a separate departmental basis. Finally devolution of administration has taken place when the regional government offices are amalgamated to form an intermediate base for the administration of central government activities.

A region may be a physical and social entity providing a homogeneity similar to, and as real as, that of the common identity which makes a nation like Wales, but in the UK the significant development of the regions has been in the creation of regions as administrative units of government, functioning at the intermediate level between local and central government.

Since 1945, the impetus for regionalisation in the UK has come from central government which, based on World War II experience, has set up a network of regions covering the whole of the UK. The network provides regional units of administration for government departments and in England they still function substantially as part of decentralised government separate departments, although there have been some moves towards the third stage of devolved administration. In Wales and Scotland, however, where there is a sense of historic national identity the two regions have had extensive devolved administration of home affairs. The process had started in Wales and Scotland well before 1945 but as will be seen in Chapter 5 much of the development in Wales is a post-war feature and has brought a measure of political devolution with the appointment of a Secretary of State to oversee the regional administration. It is partly because of the administrative devolution of wide powers that pressure has grown for a directly elected regional body to control them democratically.

While regionalisation by central government created a setting for political devolution, the political idea of a region that exists to care for a community at the intermediate level between central and local government has gained recognition as a way of governance and as an alternative to continuing centralisation.

The 'cradle to the grave' concern of the welfare state created after 1945 was matched by central control over the economy and this produced in turn its own reaction in the new regions. As part of the

16

purpose of the new society was to provide fair shares regionally, members of Parliament and local authorities in the regions, particularly the peripheral and disadvantaged—the North and North West as well as Wales and Scotland—campaigned on the basis of the region for a fair share of national resources. More recently there has also been the move to greater democratic accountability in the regions as activities of government at a regional level have been extended. In some areas regional planning, environmental protection and economic development have become issues over which there have been calls for more accountability and, in addition, the growth of quango appointments associated with the regions has strengthened the political case for regional assemblies throughout the UK.

Much of the encouragment for this increased recognition of the regions has come from Europe where previously very centralised states like France and Spain have developed new regional assemblies, in some cases with extensive powers. Many of the regions are based on historic regions, but whether old or new they have come to play a significant role in the work of the community. The European Union makes full use of the regions for its planning and delivery of services. With the establishment of the Committee of the Regions, the European institutions have acknowledged the development of regionalism and the constitutional importance of the regions as the intermediate level of government. In support of the regions the Council of Europe says that there is no reason why the growth in regions should weaken the state as the region lightens its task and enables it to concentrate on its own responsibilities.

In Wales the concentrated administrative devolution to one territorial ministry in the Welsh Office has been given its own important political dimension with the appointment of a Secretary of State for Wales, with a seat in the Cabinet. The appointment of Jim Griffiths as the first Secretary of State in 1966 was the result of his strong political campaigning on behalf of Wales. He had maintained his support for Welsh devolution through a long political career and his standing as a Labour leader ensured that the new Welsh Office brought together different government departments in Wales.

The subsequent growth in importance of the Welsh Office has led to the growth of many Welsh regional organisations, such as the Wales TUC and Wales CBI, the Welsh local authority organisations, and the voluntary bodies like Shelter. A new Welsh establishment has been created and where previously the leadership of Wales might have been cultural or even political, it has now became largely functional, concerned with the improvement of services and checking on and responding to the work of the Welsh Office.

These developments set the scene for the devolution debate that led up to the referendum in 1979. This and some of the reasons for the rejection of the proposals are looked at in Chapter 5. Times have changed. In Europe the regions have become more important and regionalism has become a term expressing the upward pressure for more recognition in Wales. There is now concern about accountability for the increasing amount of intermediate government activity by the Welsh Office and the appointments to a network of unelected bodies by the Welsh Office. Many also argue that Wales could have a better chance to move the economy from its low UK position and to present itself as a stronger region in Europe if it could have more accountable direction in an elected assembly.

There are differences within the policies of the 'opposition parties' in Wales on how an intermediate tier of democratic control would operate but they all see the need for Welsh democratic accountability. Following the General Election in 1997, the new Labour Goverment has introduced a Referendum Bill to establish a referendum to determine whether there should be a Welsh Assembly which would have the executive powers of the Welsh Office and control over the quangos. More radical proposals suggest a wide redistribution of powers from Parliament in Westminster and these are supported by Plaid Cymru and the Liberal Democrats and in the case of Plaid Cymru to seek eventually an independent Wales in Europe. In each case the proposals would give Wales a political position providing further recognition of Welsh needs and bringing it more nearly into line with most other regions in Europe. Meanwhile, the Conservative view in the run-up to the 1997 General Elections was that political accountability can properly be met by representation in the British Cabinet by the Secretary of State and in Westminster by MPs and that an elected regional body would be a threat to the unity of the British nation state.

There seems, however, no party argument against considering Wales as a region and as a nation. The dual status should be stressed. Wales is a nation because of its history and the expression of community and it is a region because it is the way in which Wales functions as part of the UK and Europe. The two characteristics overlie each other and make the position and standing similar to that in Scotland and different from the regions in England. Constitutional change has already happened more quickly in Scotland and Wales, as with the scale of administrative devolution to the two nation-regions, and this looks set to continue. It is reasonable to see Wales as a nation-region with its modern functions and status enhanced by its character as a historic nation. If there is an elected assembly, the work that it will do as a region, exercising regional functions, should not be substantially different from that of elected regional assemblies elsewhere in Europe, but its work will be done in the special Welsh context as a nation-region.

References and further reading:

Archer & Butler, *The European Community. Structure & Process*, 1992, Pinter.
V. Bogdanor, 'Europe, subsidiarity and the British Constitution', 1994, *R.S.A Journal.*
V. Bogdanor, *Devolution*, 1979, O.U.P.
G. Carey, *On being European*, 1993, CAFE.
Church in Wales, *Wales in Europe, Core or Periphery*, 1992, Church in Wales.
R. Coupland, *Welsh and Scottish Nationalism*, 1954, Collins.
E.J. Hobsbawm, *Nations and Nationalism since 1780*, 1990, Cambridge.
Hogwood & Keating, *Regional Government in England*, 1982, Clarendon.
Madgwick and Rowe, *The territorial dimension in UK politics*, 1982, Macmillan.
K.O. Morgan, *Rebirth of a Nation, Wales 1880-1980*, 1981, University of Wales.
John Osmond, *The democratic challenge*, 1992, Gomer.
Dai Smith, *Wales!Wales?*, 1984, George Allen and Unwin.
Trentino Conference: *Regional Diversity in Europe*, 1993, ECTARC.
George Thomas, *My Wales*, 1986, Century.
Gwyn A. Williams, *When was Wales?*, 1985, Penguin.

Chapter 2

WELSH NATIONALITY

A nation depends upon an understanding of its history, even where the history is a short one. In Wales's case the history can be traced back way beyond the formation of the English nation and in this chapter an outline of some aspects of the long history of Wales is given in the hope that it will help make sense of the present. Some parts of this history relate to events that took place over a thousand years ago but are mentioned because of possible relevance to the shaping of modern Wales. It might be worth adding at this point that it is not possible to create a nation solely out of the ancient past and while its former history is helpful in identifying the nature of a modern nation, it should not be used to establish a nation which no longer exists.

For many, the sense of belonging to a nation arises from more recent shared events like the identification with radical politics or participation in sport. It is possible to create, in a short space of time, a strong national identity directly from a struggle for freedom or other cause—as happened in the United States in its fight for independence.

Nation formation can develop and manifest itself in many different ways. This chapter attempts to provide the context in which the Welsh nation evolved.

TERRITORY: THE LAND OF MY FATHERS

The physical boundaries of a nation provide it with its definite area and without them there is no distinct territory to which the language, race, culture or other social attitude is related. They connect the people to the territory, whether the people live within the area or are living away from 'home'. Wales's boundaries have been formed over the centuries and are part of the historical development of both Britain and Wales.

EARLY DEFINITION OF BOUNDARIES

The Celtic people known as the Brythons or Britons resisted the Romans, kept their own language, Cumbric, which was an old form of what has become modern Welsh, and when the Romans left at the end of the fourth century are said to have led the whole of Britain south of the River Clyde. For three hundred years these people grouped into clans (*cenedl*) and shared in a Romano-Celtic heritage, resisting attacks from the Picts in the north and the Saxons from the east. It is a period more remembered in legend than history—in stories like Hengist and the Treason of the Long Knives and the most persistent of all the legends, that of King Arthur. The poems of sixth-century bards Taliesin and Aneurin who came from yr Hen Ogledd (the Old North which is now southern Scotland and northern England and Wales) tell of the tribes that made up the old country and of attacks from the east by Anglo-Saxons. In one poem, which can be read in translation in the *Oxford Book of Welsh Verse*, Aneurin recounts how the Gododdin from around Edinburgh fought alongside other Britons, including a contingent from Gwynedd, at Catterick in Yorkshire, but were defeated by the invaders.

The continuity of the country between north and south Britain was broken in 615 by Aethelfrich and after the slaughter of several hundred monks of the old Celtic Church at Bangor on Dee, his victory at the Battle of Chester was decisive in severing the ancient British nation. The southern part included what is now Wales.

WALLIA ALONE

In the two centuries that followed the battle of Chester, the country of the Britons became known variously as Cambria or Cymru (which means fellow country man) or Wallia or Wales (which means foreigner and was the term used by invaders) and the extent of the country was eventually consolidated with the land border near the present boundary. After centuries of resistance, the old British frontier was fixed by reference to a boundary marked out by a continuous constructed dyke known as Offa's Dyke (Clawdd Offa). It takes its name from King Offa (757-779), king of Mercia, who ruled over several minor chieftains covering the whole of what is now the Midlands of England, and had control over the area east of Wales, extending from the River Severn in the south to the River Dee in the north. Penalties were imposed for crossing the border which came clearly to mark out the area that is Wales. The area around the boundary, both to the east and west, remained under dispute and was fought over until the thirteenth century. The part that became Tegeingel or Flintshire, and is now to the east of Clawdd Offa was, for instance, won back into Wales in 796 but continued to be a disputed area until the Welsh boundary ceased to be a military frontier and what was Flintshire was made formally part of Wales.

Clawdd Offa remains as the nominal boundary, although it is now several miles within Wales in north Wales and in some places crosses into England. It is commemorated by the long distance footpath that extends from north to south Wales.

PRE-NORMAN DIVISION OF WALES

While the area of Cymru came to be identified by reference to the land west of Clawdd Offa, within Wales itself the country existed as a collection of kingdoms, which were themselves loose assemblies of clans. The number and locations of the kingdoms in Wales varied from time to time. According to Sir John Lloyd, there were three kingdoms—Gwynedd, Powys and Deheubarth, with Gwent and Morganwg coming into existence later in the period separately from Deheubarth. More recent writers identify more kingdoms but the main picture is of a country 'of many kings, many dynasties, many kingdoms' (Professor R.R. Davies).

THE NORMAN INVASION

The Welsh had met the Anglo Saxons' attacks in the east around the line of Clawdd Offa and had also dealt with Viking/Norse attacks on their coasts, but in the eleventh century, the Norman/French conquest of England brought new challenges to the territory of Wales. William the Conqueror laid claim to overlordship of Wales and built castles at Chester, Shrewsbury and Hereford. One of his barons, Robert of Rhuddlan, advanced to Deganwy in the north, while in south Wales the Normans advanced as far as Pembrokeshire. They occupied parts of Wales through the use of adventurous and ruthless barons who were given the lordships of land in return for their efforts in extending the conquest of England beyond the boundary (the March) of Wales. Along the north and south Wales coasts and along the eastern border, the Marcher Lords ruled over Border (Marcher) Wales. Native Wales (Wallia Pura) remained a collection of kingdoms and clans which resisted the invasion and occasionally united to fight back and recover land taken by the Norman/French. For a time, Native Wales was united under Llywelyn I—Llywelyn the Great (d.1240) who presided at Councils as the Prince of Wales and through support of some of the English barons in England against their King John obtained special provisions for Wales in the Magna Carta (including the return of lands held in Wales by King John). Llywelyn's grandson, Llywelyn II, obtained the Principality of Wales from Henry III and again received the acknowledgement of the ownership of lands he had retaken from some of the Marcher Lords.

EDWARDIAN CONQUEST

The Edwardian conquest that followed the defeat of Llywelyn II claimed the subordination of Native Wales (Walia Pura). Wales was, by the terms of the Statute of Wales or Rhuddlan 1284, wholly and entirely transferred—'annexed and united' to England by King Edward. Castles were built at Conwy, Caernarfon and elsewhere and the part of Wales not in the Marcher Lordships was incorporated into the English structure of local government. Six shires were created over the area of Native Wales following older Welsh kingdoms—these were Anglesey, Caernarfonshire, Merionethshire, Camarthenshire, Cardiganshire and Flintshire. The rest remained under the occupation of the Marcher Lords, although Pembrokeshire and Glamorgan later became Palatine counties having direct loyalty to the crown. The counties of Wales were to become the basis by which the boundary was determined, although not finally settled until the sixteenth century with the completion of the county network in Wales.

Even with the claimed subordination of Wales by Edward I, it was left culturally separate and Welsh law remained in force for more than a century. It was a policy of accommodation that was broken only by Owain Glyndŵr's rebellion in 1400, and the repression that followed his defeat. Owain planned to extend the boundaries of Wales but the period of independence that he brought did not result in changes in the frontier, which had now been largely fixed. Owain's defeat must have seemed the end of any prospect of ever recovering land to the east of

Wales. But at the end of the century a change in dynastic fortunes in England revived the dream of the reconquest of Britain by the Welsh.

THE ACTS OF UNION

Henry VII was grandson of Owain ap Meredudd ap Tudor—he adopted the name Owen or Owain Tudor—and his family were kinsmen of Owain Glyndŵr. Henry had been brought up to speak Welsh and when he landed in Milford Haven in 1485 to claim the English crown for the Lancastrian cause the Welsh rallied to support him in battle. His victory over Richard III at Bosworth led to the general belief in Wales that the ancient prophecies of recapture of the old Britain by the Welsh had been fulfilled and that Henry had come to 'tame the Saxon'. Henry and the Tudor dynasty that he started had different ideas for they were monarchs of England and Wales and the court was in London.

There were, however, plenty of Welsh supporters at the court and the Tudors rewarded them for their services. Apart from the grant of positions in court itself, disabilities on holding office and restrictions on using English law were reduced or removed. In response to requests from many leaders in Wales, new legislation was brought in by Henry VIII to establish this integration and the most important was the Act of Union 1536, or strictly the Acts of Union, as there was one act in 1536 and another in 1542.

These statutes further fixed the territory of Wales by abolishing the Marcher (Border) Lordships, which were replaced by new shire counties—Denbighshire, Radnorshire, Montgomery, Brecon and Monmouthshire—and were brought under English administration. These counties, which were added to the previously created counties and followed the boundaries of the old Marcher Lordships, were not fixed by a reference to community of interest. As a result of keeping to Marcher boundaries, Shrewsbury, where more Welsh was then spoken than English, and Hereford, which was the centre of the south Wales market, were not included in the new county structure of Wales. Neither were all the Marcher Lordships included in Wales but some were added to English counties and as a consequence Oswestry went into Shropshire and Archenfield went to Herefordshire.

The Acts of Union did not join England and Wales. The annexation was assumed to have taken place in 1284 or before and the Tudor Acts dealt with the acceptance of Wales as part of the new Tudor nation as well as such consequential matters as the creation of the new counties, the drawing of the boundaries, the administration of the courts, the application of English law, the right to representation in Westminster, and the appointment of justices of the peace. Professor Glanmor Williams says that what was new was that all the King's subjects 'should henceforth enjoy freedoms and laws as his subjects in England'. The Tudors may not have taken England for the Welsh cause, but Henry VII legitimated the Union because he was Welsh, had Welsh support and he and his son, Henry VIII, gave the Welsh what their leaders then most wanted: equality with the English.

The territory of Wales has remained tied to the counties through the centuries since the Act of Union. Even with the new reorganisation of local government and the creation of eleven counties and eleven county boroughs as unitary authorities under the Local Government (Wales) Act 1994, (see appendix) the boundary between England and Wales is still defined by reference to the area of the counties as defined in 1974, which in turn related back to the Tudor settlement of the boundaries of Wales. While the Tudors did not enlarge the area of Wales, they provided it with a definition which has lasted through four hundred years.

As the Welsh boundary follows the county boundaries, the only disputes since 1536 have been a matter for the counties to resolve. This happened in the early 1970s when there was dispute between Flintshire and Cheshire over the boundary between the counties lying in the estuary of the River Dee. The issue might have been important if some proposed land reclamation in the Dee estuary had gone ahead. The boundary had been assumed for ordnance survey purposes to follow the centre line in the estuary, but Cheshire claimed that it should be nearer to the Welsh coast lying close to the town of Flint. The claim was the subject of a counterclaim by Flintshire that an Act of 1732 had the effect of bringing the boundary to the line which was the centre of the channel of the Dee in existence at the time in 1725. This was before the river was canalised from Queensferry to Chester and the counterclaim would have taken the boundary close to the Cheshire coast. The claim and counterclaim were overtaken by the 1974 reorganisation of local government and the issue never reached

25

court so that the middle line of the estuary is still taken as the nominal boundary.

The definition of boundaries in the estuaries and around the coasts of Wales may still be of significance if there is land reclamation in the future or with the discovery of valuable resources on the sea bed.

TERRITORIAL MINISTRIES

While the boundary has been fixed for four centuries and the land to which the Welsh belong clearly defined, the development of the Welsh Office has brought Wales into focus as a regionally defined unit. It has led to the mapping of Wales as a region of the UK and Europe and the existence of the Welsh Office, with the same territory as that covered by the geographic area of the counties, has given the Welsh boundary a new economic and social significance. Those involved in the services for which the Welsh Office are responsible, as both providers and consumers, have been placed within Wales—those using Welsh hospitals are Welsh patients, Welsh economic development is essential for Welsh employers and Welsh workers and Welsh schools provide education for Welsh school-children and so on. The territorial importance of being Welsh is possibly greater than it has been since before the Tudors because the Welsh Office has placed residence as the test for being Welsh for the purposes of government. In the execution of its regional functions the historic area of Wales has been adopted by the Welsh Office and the same is true of the recognition of the boundaries of Wales as a region in Europe by the European Union. In both cases the drawing of the boundaries along the historic line is consistent with the existence of Wales as a nation-region and makes a contribution towards its development.

THE HISTORIC FOUNDATIONS

Wales has had centuries of history during which the foundations of modern Welsh identity were formed. The territorial definition of boundaries set the framework but distinctively, and within the historical framework already given in this chapter, it is possible to trace the historic basis through at least its laws, its religion and its language.

National identity in Scotland has been said by Sir Reginald Coupland to have three pillars—the separate Law of Scotland, the Kirk, which is the established Church of Scotland, and the old Parliament, which was surrendered by the 1707 Act of Union and this foundation is sometimes presented as a reason why Scotland should be treated differently from Wales in preparing any plan for devolution. There may be claimed for Wales a similar triple grounding for its national identity—perhaps not so institutionalised but as historically relevant. The historic foundations for Wales may be described as the separate Laws of Wales (which were finally surrendered by the 1536 Act of Union), the Christian religion in Wales and the ancient Celtic language. A brief look at their history will show their importance in the formation of Wales as it is and as it is remembered. As in Scotland, the historic foundations are discernible even after generations of change.

1. THE LAWS OF WALES

In Wales a separate system of laws existed for something like a thousand years and is remembered and linked with the name of the king called Hywel Dda (920-950)—the only Welsh Prince given the title 'Good', a title given because of his work in the codification of the Laws of Wales. He set down the existing laws and customs, which had governed Welsh tribal society for centuries, into a consistent and uniform system to be adopted throughout the whole country. This identification of Wales with a national jurisprudence was given common backing with an Assembly at Whitland in Dyfed in 942 to settle the codification of the Laws. The Assembly might be said to have been the first Welsh Parliament: six representatives were called from each district in Wales and they had to stay in session until all was agreed. The Laws provided that they should only be changed by a similar assembly meeting together.

Legend has it that Hywel also took the Laws to Rome for a papal blessing but although the records show that Hywel did visit Rome on a pilgrimage, it preceded the Assembly meeting and, in any case, it is unlikely that the Church would have approved the Laws. The Laws reflected the customs of Wales and some of them would have been contrary to the powerful Roman Church Law—in particular, Welsh

Laws regarded marriage more as a contract than a permanent status of subordination for women. And divorce, although unacceptable to the Church, was permitted in Wales under the Welsh Laws if the wife was properly provided for. A different regard for the family in Welsh Laws also appeared in the provision that married women retained some rights within their own clan after marriage and Welsh Laws did not distinguish between the rights of natural and lawful children if the illegitimate child had been acknowledged by the family.

Hywel's work was particularly important because he set down the laws that bound the tribes and clans of Wales together and because the Laws provide detailed information about the structure of that native society. Some of the dynasties who ruled the tribes came from Roman times and their importance was reflected in the importance given in the Welsh Laws to the Chief or King who ruled over the tribes, sometimes uniting through marriage or force of arms to form a kingdom. Starting from the top of society with the prince, the Welsh Laws recognised that status was fundamental at each level and set out the relationship between Lord and subject and also between freemen and strangers and slaves. Gwyn A. Williams points out that the native Welsh society was built on the backs of the unfree and 'it looks as though there were plenty of them'.

The king was at the head of the tribe but the basic social organisation among freemen depended upon an extended family which was the clan, *cenedl*—the word now used commonly for 'nation'— and the clan was led by an elder elected for life by the heads of households in the clan. Membership of the clan depended upon common descent of males from a common great grandfather, or in some areas the great greatgrandfather, and it is clear that tracing descent was very important. In most cases people cherished their family trees as a point of honour and as was seen by Geraldus Cambrensis, 'Even the common people know their family trees by heart and can readily recite from memory the list of their ancestors . . . back to the sixth or seventh generation', (quoted by Professor R.R. Davies). With the use of the patronymic form the identification of kinsmen established an emphasis upon family ties that helped bind the Welsh together. In any case, as a form of basic law enforcement, the clan was responsible for meeting the compensation value (*galanas*) for an injury caused by one of the clan. Descent was also important in the larger social group—the tribe—but it appears likely that in this descent group it was of less real significance and represented only acknowledgement of some family association within the tribe and of its head, the lord, chief or king. Sir John Lloyd suggested that the tribal association was known as the *cantref*, although recent work suggests a different relationship between the *cenedl* and the *cantref*.

Our existing copies of the Welsh Laws were written down almost three centuries later than the time of Hywel: the first of them was the Black Book of Chirk (so called because it was owned by John Edwards of Chirk in the seventeenth century) and that copy dates from the time when Llywelyn I (Llywelyn the Great) entered in to the treaty with King John of England to respect the integrity of the Welsh Laws (Lex Wallia) and the Laws may have been written up for this purpose.

Although codified in the tenth century by Hywel, the Welsh Laws were modified over the centuries by the jurists, and the Black Book of Chirk includes some of the changes that had taken place by that date. The changes were not, however, sufficient to meet the needs of a changing society. They provided for a society in which each community was largely self-sufficient and the land laws proved particularly inadequate. The emphasis upon the descent group meant that even freemen held only a life interest in land. Normally it could not be sold or devised on death and it passed from generation to generation, being shared on death among direct male heirs (sons and grandsons) equally under the principle of gavelkind (*cyfran*). This basic law gave proper respect to the family but did not meet the needs of society when it began to benefit from trade. The absence of any process for the review of the Laws, together with the absence of provision of documentary title relating to land and the attractiveness of the developing common law of England, built up the pressures for change. It was a pressure for change that seems to have come from within Wales and not by imposition.

Slowly English law was introduced—in the criminal law there were petitions in the twelfth century for the introduction of the jury system into Marcher Wales and by the end of the fourteenth century it seems that the English Common Law was widely used in Wales. The transfer was completed by the Acts of Union in 1536-42 and English Common Law replaced what was referred to in the Acts as part of 'the sinister usages and customs of Wales'.

The Laws had been important in forming the nation and continued to remain as a part of the collective history of the people. They had bound the tribes together, created an agreed constitution, and provided an emphasis upon the family which was not adequately matched by English Law in some respects until the present century. Social and economic change made a radical break necessary and the Tudors provided legislation to conclude the process of transfer.

There was no provision for the continuation of separate law-making in Wales and any special statutory provision for Wales would be a matter for Westminster. There were some acts of parliament affecting Wales—the Act of 1563 requiring the bishops of Wales and Hereford to provide a Welsh translation of the Bible and Prayer Book and in 1650, during the time of the Commonwealth, the Act for the Better Propagation and Preaching of the Gospel in Wales. Thereafter there was no such general legislation for Wales until the Sunday Observance Act 1881. It remains to be seen whether there will be any devolved legislative powers to a future assembly for Wales, but if there were to be law-making powers it might provide the opportunity for a new start in a distinctive Welsh jurisprudence in matters of contemporary concern to the people of Wales.

The form of administration of justice in the country is another part of a country's jurisprudence and here the Act of Union 1536 provided a new court system for Wales based upon a distinctive and separate court called the Court of Great Sessions. The Law that it administered, however, was that of England and, apart from a very few rules, such as the civil action to recover debt, so too was its procedure. Most of its judges were English-speaking and while Gwyn A. Williams found that a largely 'monoglot people were made alien in their own courts', there is evidence referred to below that for some time after the Acts of Union Welsh could also be heard in the courts. The Court of Great Sessions continued as a form of devolved administration until it was abolished in 1830—when improved transport appeared to make the separate court unnecessary.

The administration of justice in Wales after the abolition of the Great Sessions still maintained some of its distinctive Welsh character. There was a Welsh circuit of the Court on Assize, which did not include Monmouth but included Chester and when the Assize Court was replaced by the Crown Court system in 1972 a presiding judge was provided for the Welsh circuit, which now does include Monmouthshire. Under the terms of the Welsh Language Act 1967, the principle of equal validity for Welsh with English was at last recognised and marked another distinctive procedural form for the Welsh courts. Devolution provisions might also include new structure for the courts in Wales and the proposals in the report of Judge Watkin Powell suggested a Welsh Section of the Supreme Court.

Although not part of the judiciary, provision for remedies against administrative decisions is made today through tribunals under statutory provisions, and not the least of these is the office of Welsh Ombudsman appointed to deal with administrative complaints in relation to local government in Wales. The concept behind the creation of the office represented progress in control of administrative decisions and its Welsh commission again reflected a territorial recognition of Wales in administration.

These administrative provisions have helped to maintain some Welsh identity in the law in Wales, but the substantive law is that of the Common Law together with Westminster statutes, supplemented more recently by that of the European Union under the European Communities Act 1972. Substantive Welsh Law, unlike the Scottish legal provisions, is a matter of history but its existence in the past has helped shape Wales and, as will be discussed later, may still be relevant in determining Wales's status as a nation rather than a region.

2. RELIGION

The Acts of Union might well have led to the complete assimilation of Wales into England, in which case Wales could have become a historic memory. The earlier existence of the Welsh Laws would almost certainly not have been sufficient in itself to sustain Welsh identity and it was the other historic foundations of Welsh identity, the religion and the language, that continued to bind Wales as a separate country. In this review of Welsh history, religion means the Christian religion and the church is taken as the organisational form of the Christian religion in Wales in both church and chapel. In this context religion, as will be seen, has been a major contributor to the creation of Welsh consciousness in both the earliest and most recent periods and each period has continuing impact upon the country today.

One of the legends that developed in the later Middle Ages about the beginnings of Christianity in Wales was that it was introduced in the first century mission of Cynfelin, the father of Caractacus (Caradoc), on his return from Rome. This has the sound of historical accuracy but, apart from the legend there is no evidence for it; the likely history is that the first preaching of the gospel came to Britain around 400AD, as part of the monastic movement away from the increasingly prosperous church around the Mediterranean and it brought with it traditions different from that of the main Western church.

The early Celtic church in Wales had close contacts with the church in Brittany and Cornwall and flourished while the rest of Europe followed the Roman Empire in retreat. It was, with the Celtic Church in Scotland and Ireland, the 'one great light in a great darkness' (G.M. Trevelyan quoted by Coupland).

The age of the Welsh Saints—David, Illtud, Cadog, Deiniol and others who are still remembered in Wales—is significant in any consideration of Welsh identity. They brought in a monastic form of worship based on the *llan* which could indicate both a church or an enclosure within which were the monks' cells, as well as the church, the hospice and other buildings (Sir John Lloyd). Here everything was held in common in a community headed by the abbot, sometimes called a bishop. He was chosen either by the community itself or by the local chieftain who supported the monastery, and, generally, the religious community reflected the local tribal community.

When St Augustine landed in Kent in 597 for the conversion of England to Christianity, there were already bishops in Wales who were located in what were to become cathedral sees. Attempts made to bring uniformity between the Celtic Church in Wales and the Church at Canterbury were resisted and the meeting between Roman envoys of St Augustine and seven Welsh bishops and monks from Bangor on Dee failed to bring the churches together. It was assumed that there were no longer any theological differences as those that had previously existed seem to have been resolved when a previous envoy—Germanus of Auxerre (St Garmon)—visited Wales in the early fifth century.

The Welsh Church refused to accept Augustine as Archbishop and continued to maintain its own practice of baptism and its own Church calendar which it continued to do until the last part of the eighth century. The Welsh Church, moreover, was so linked to its tribal community that it was unwilling to accept a further request to develop a mission to the pagan outside Wales. The Church identified with the native society's resistance to the Anglo-Saxon invaders and the need was seen to be to preserve what was Welsh rather than convert the enemy. 'From birth they lived under the threat of extinction', (Gwyn A. Williams) and the Welsh relied on the religious backing of the local church to maintain their separate way of life.

The Welsh Church shared in the teachings of other Celtic saints like Patrick, Columba and Kentigern so that when Kentigern was driven from Strathclyde he went to north-east Wales and established the monastery at St Asaph (Llanelwy). Although the theology of the Celtic Church might have been acceptable to Canterbury, there is evidence that within their tradition they maintained a particular concern for spirituality. The Celtic lessons about the enjoyment of God's world and the wonder of God in nature have been acknowleged in recent times and again form a valued contribution to Christian thinking.

Whatever the extent of direct Welsh participation in this tradition, there is no doubt about the identification of the Church with the Welsh people from the beginning of their self-awareness. It survived many military and political changes in the first millenium and provided Wales with some stability.

The Norman conquest from the eleventh century brought controls which dismantled the old monastaries and brought the dismissal of some of its saints—in those churches around the Norman Castles. The church was brought more firmly under papal authority and the control of Canterbury. New European orders of monks replaced the old Celtic orders and the establishment, by 1150, of four dioceses covering Wales, the building of new churches and abbeys and the creation of a network of parishes were all effective signs of the conquest by the Normans.

The conquest was, however, not without advantages to Christian religion—integration with the European church brought new cultural and religious influences, including the opportunity to copy Latin, French and Welsh documents. The new abbeys and their libraries provided the means to copy in Welsh the Laws and the Mabinogion stories and to copy Welsh literature and legends into Latin and French.

The churchmen may have been Cambro-Norman but they worked to establish the position of the new church in Wales. The Cistercians in particular became naturalised very rapidly—and were accused by the Norman and English Kings of stirring up the nationalist cause. Giraldus Cambrensis, Gerald the Welshman (1146-1223) led a campaign for an independent metropolitan archbishop of Wales but this failed because the English recognised that to yield metropolitan status to St David's was a recipe for 'perpetual dissension between the English and the Welsh' (R.R. Davies). As a reaction to the continental influence now surrounding the church, David became recognised as the patron saint of the whole of Wales and he and other Celtic saints were canonised by the Roman church.

FROM THE TUDORS TO THE REVIVAL

The Tudor accession at the end of the fifteenth century brought assimilation into the ways of England nearer because of their attraction to the leaders of Welsh society. The Tudor Church of the Reformation was English and the translation of the Bible into the Welsh language was approved by Queen Elizabeth I because it was seen as a way of encouraging the use of the Reformed Prayer Book in English. It was argued to the Westminster authorities that a Welsh language bible would make it far easier for those able to speak only Welsh to understand the English scriptures and would be an intermediate step to the common use of English, encouraging people to support the Protestant cause.

William Salesbury (1520-1584) of Llansannan, using some of the language of the old Welsh Laws, wrote a Welsh translation of the Epistles and Gospels and of the Book of Common Prayer and, with Bishop Richard Davies, was responsible for the Act of Parliament in 1563 which authorised the translation of the Bible into Welsh. The Bible was largely translated by Davies and Salesbury but credit for the completion of the work goes to Bishop William Morgan of St Asaph. The purpose of the Welsh translation was to ensure support in Wales for the Tudor Reformation, and although 'some gentry remained Catholic until the eighteenth century, more than anything else, it rooted the Reforming faith among the Welsh' (*Oxford Companion to the Literature of Wales, OCLW*). It did not, however, return the Church to the Welsh community. This did not happen until the Revival, when the translation of the Bible was made available to the Welsh people 'in their cottages' (Coupland).

Although the English Church remained dominant in Wales until the Methodist Revival, the Puritans and the old dissenting denominations became important in Wales, particularly during the Civil War in the middle of the seventeenth century. While the leaders of Wales were mainly royalist supporters, leading dissenters like Morgan Llwyd in Wrexham came both to preach the gospel and support the Parliamentary cause. During the period of the Commonwealth, Wales was for religious purposes treated by the Commonwealth as a separate nation. Under the Act for the Better Propagation of the Gospel in Wales, 1650, there was an autonomous structure under Colonel Thomas Harrison, with preachers like Morgan Llwyd preaching and converting in the north and Vavasor Powell in the south (Geraint Jenkins). The puritan teaching was to provide much of the basis for the preaching of the Revival of the eighteenth century.

THE WELSH REVIVAL

Although the revival of religion in Wales in the eighteenth century was to be linked with nonconformity, it started within the established church as an attempt to meet the educational needs of the poor. Following earlier campaigns, Griffith Jones (1683-1761) an Anglican vicar and member of the SPCK (the Society for the Propagation of Christian Knowledge) combined the distribution of bibles in Welsh with the establishment of charity schools of a special kind. Known as circulating schools, they even caught the attention of Catherine the Great of Russia after her envoy had reported on their success. The schools were a form of distance learning based upon a short term stay at farms in the winter when there was less farm work to be done. Some three thousand such schools were set up in Griffith Jones's lifetime and 160,000 people were taught to read.

The new Welsh literacy and the subsequent use of the Welsh Bible provided a basis for a religious revival, paralleled a few years later in England by that of the Wesleys. The Welsh Revival was led by Hywel Harris (1714-73), who travelled around Wales preaching salvation and affecting the lives of the common people with an emotional appeal in the language that the ordinary people of Wales could understand. Harris, with his colleagues, was involved in a movement which at the end of the eighteenth century saw the need to break away from the Church of England. A separate denomination was eventually established in 1811 called the Calvinistic Methodist Church (and more recently the Presbyterian Church of Wales). It was Calvinist in outlook, reflecting Harris's association with George Whitfield on a mission in America, and Presbyterian in organisation and so led both by ministers and elders. It was a church of the common people and became the church to which most of the Welsh people adhered in the nineteenth century.

Early Calvinistic Methodism established a Bible-based community and the arrival of bibles in a village was a cause of great excitement. Sunday Schools for children and adults were common and became important in extending literacy as well as scriptural knowledge. By the middle of the nineteenth century this indigenous Welsh church was strong and confident enough to join the missionary endeavours of the time and a Welsh mission church was established in north-east India, which has continued in a separate form to the present time—and now has a very much larger membership than the parent church.

The Welsh Calvinistic Methodist Church created a spiritual society, similar to movements in America. It was an enthusiastic hymn-singing religion, and, without becoming or seeking to become the established church of Wales, it also spoke for the conscience of the country. Even with the decline in religious organisations, the nonconformist churches had in 1990 more members (220,000) than the Anglican (110,000) and Roman Catholic (60,000) churches combined, although most of the nonconformist members are now outside the Calvinistic Methodist church (53,000 members in 1994) and include many of an evangelical or pentecostal tradition.

In the second half of the nineteenth century, Welsh Calvinistic Methodists and other nonconformists in Wales were moved to engage in political action. It was mainly a reaction against the attack on the Welsh language and the nonconformist church by government commissioners in 1847 (the Treason of the Blue Books) and, as will be seen, was directed almost exclusively at what were seen as the Welsh nonconformist causes: education, temperance, Sunday Observance and disestablishment.

From the time of the Reformation, the Church of England was distant from the Welsh-speaking majority in Wales and was seen as the Church of the English and landed gentry. There was no Welsh-speaking bishop appointed between 1715 and 1870 and many of the vicars were absent and not Welsh-speaking. For many tenant farmers the payment of tithes as a land duty to the established Church made disestablishment a particularly important cause for nonconformists. Eventually, through the Liberal Nonconformist political ascendancy in Wales, the Disestablishment Act 1914 led to the creation of the Anglican Church in Wales, with the Archbishop of Wales at its head.

The disestablishment of the Church of England in Wales has had important consequences for the country. A bitterly divisive issue in Wales at the time, the verdict on the change from a prominent Welsh Wesleyan methodist, George Thomas, is that since disestablishment the Anglican church has gone from strength to strength in Wales. 'It has stolen the clothes of the nonconformists' in taking on the role of speaking out on social issues for the people of Wales as a whole. With the decline in the proportion of people speaking Welsh, the still predominately Welsh-speaking Calvinistic Methodist Church often seems to reflect the conscience of and speak for a smaller part of the population. Whether or not this is correct, disestablishment has certainly made Wales different from both England and Scotland in that there is no established church in Wales and the Episcopalian Church in Wales, as in Scotland, stands free of the state commitment of the Church of England.

Since the Second World War, the efforts of the churches in Wales have been towards renewal by covenanting for unity and the aspiration is for a United Church of Wales, at least incorporating the Church in Wales (Anglican), Presbyterian (Calvinistic Methodist), United Reformed, Methodist (Wesleyan) and some Baptist churches. Both the Church in Wales and the Presbyterian Church of Wales have well established Welsh institutional structures and the alienation that caused this division in the eighteenth century no longer exists. Progress to covenanted union has, however, been slow and recently there has been revived talk of a united Welsh Free (nonconformist) Church. The ecumenical movement in Wales has been organised by the Welsh Council of Churches, now named Cytun (Together) and has become a distinctive part of Welsh life. The various denominations have yet to build a new church which can overcome language as well as ecclesiastical differences but in the Welsh setting, religion has generally been responsive to the needs of the community and is still a part of the distinctive Welsh culture.

3. LANGUAGE

Closely linked to the religion of Wales is the Welsh language which is the third of the historic foundations of Welsh nationality. At the beginning of the nineteenth century the language was still spoken by most Welsh people, but with social change, immigration and the decline in Welsh nonconformity its position has weakened. By the end of the nineteenth century the Welsh-speaking population had fallen to half the population of Wales and this was followed by a further decline in succeeding decades, with real fears for its continued existence. A recent change of attitude to the language by the majority of people in Wales, both Welsh and non Welsh speakers, may have brought a halt to the decline and it is at present possibly recovering from its lowest position, when only 20% speak Welsh.

WELSH LANGUAGE FROM THE MIDDLE AGES

Although native Welsh society was made up of differing and often warring tribes, it shared a common language and a common bardic tradition. They complemented the bonds created by the Welsh Laws and the Welsh Church and together they created a strong sense of common unity alongside a highly particularised local identity. The language was an essential requirement for membership of any tribe, and those not speaking it were taken to be alien. The bards used the language to celebrate the whole of Wales and, while praising their own tribal chiefs and claiming a descent for them from the famous Romano-British families, they made imaginary journeys of praise beyond the boundaries of their own tribe. They freely made use of the stories of Arthur and the Celtic traditions of Aneurin and Taliesin and, although none of these were born in what is now Wales, they became the heroes of the poetic tradition in Wales.

When the Norman-French invaded Wales, the presence of another language made the Welsh very conscious of their own distinct and separate language, especially because they sensed the continuous threat of assimilation. The new people in Wales were often of mixed Norman and Welsh (and in some places English and Flemish) families:one of them was Geoffrey of Monmouth (1090-1155) who wrote the history of this island—Yr Ynys Prydain. In his *Kings of Britain*, he gave the first written collection of stories about Arthur and provided the basis for the widespread following of Arthur that appeared throughout Western Europe. Geoffrey and the other great Cambro-Norman writer, Giraldus Cambrensis (1146-1223), wrote in Latin but they were later translated into Welsh and strengthened the Welsh identity at a time when the nation was under threat from the conquest.

Gerald's father was a Norman but, on his mother's side, he was descended from the kings of Dehcubarth. He wrote about Wales and provided in his *Journey in Wales* 'an incomparable picture of life of twelfth-century Wales', (Coupland). He, too, wrote of the whole country although it was now split into Walia Pura (native Wales) and the March of Wales—the division of one people into two societies had already begun: English/Flemish and Norman/French in the towns, and Native Welsh in the countryside—the pattern in both Walia Pura and Marcher Wales. The language of Wales, however, remained Welsh, and, from 1284 to 1485, in a society which was increasingly under English political and economic influence, it was still possible for Welsh poetry to flourish. The greatest of Welsh mediaeval poets, Dafydd ap Gwilym (1325-1380), developed new forms of verse and incorporating European literary concepts wrote for the Marcher Lords, Welsh princes and the abbots of Cistercian houses.

FROM THE ACT OF UNION TO THE REVIVAL

The Tudor accession obviously had a great effect on Wales but it did not ban, as is sometimes argued, the use of Welsh. It remained the language of the people of Wales and retained a semi-official status. The records show that the language was used at the trial of Richard Gwyn, Catholic convert and martyr in 1582, and that the Presiding Judge was Welsh-speaking. Welsh was also used in administrative matters in the King's Council of Wales and the Marches, which had been established in 1509. English had, however, become the official language of administration, law and business, (P.R. Roberts in the *Cymmrodorion Transactions*) and anyone wishing to hold office or conduct business needed to speak English. It had also become the language of the property-owning class, although most of those who remained in Wales, and did not seek preferment in London, continued to speak the Welsh language as well. Even among those who went to England, the Welsh language must have been common for, according to an anecdote repeated from a collection of stories in England in 1567, when St Peter was worn out by the sound of the Welsh in heaven, he went outside the pearly gates and 'cried with a loud voice, *"Caws pob"*—that is as much as to say "roasted cheese" which thing the Welshmen hearing, ran out of heaven', because of the love of the Welsh for cheese.

Within the Church the translations of the Bible and the Book of Common Prayer into Welsh became available for use in church services, but for the most part the result of the Reformation was to replace Latin with English as the language of services thus alienating those congregations who could not speak English. Similarly in the arts the use of English became common—less than half the books published and written by Welsh men were in Welsh. The poet Henry Vaughan (1621-95) was Welsh-speaking but wrote in English and referred to himself as a writer in a more civilised language. There were some important exceptions such as the Wrexham minister, author and poet, Morgan Llwyd (1619-59) who wrote mainly in Welsh and it is said that at his best his prose 'is unequalled in Welsh' (*OCLW*). Generally, however, the poetic culture that had flourished in the middle ages disappeared under the social pressures of the Tudor success.

During the two centuries following the Act of Union, the life of the majority in Wales remained simple, poor, illiterate and non-English speaking and when the people of Wales became literate, they did so in the native Welsh language, and then mainly because of the existence of the Welsh Bible and the advent of the Welsh Methodist Revival.

Griffith Jones and the circulating schools laid the foundation for the Revival which brought a spiritual awakening to the people, and with it new life to the Welsh language. It brought literacy through the bible-based enthusiasm of the Welsh community itself. The translation of the Bible became the means of language and cultural development as well as spiritual revival. It produced great preachers and poets like William Williams Pantycelyn (1717-91), whose hymn-writing brought 'rare immediacy and symbolic richness' (*OCLW*) to religious passion. It also provided the base for the enthusiasm for teaching among Welsh people—the Welsh language was used for a teaching based upon worship and Bible study.

Although not a nationalist movement the Methodist Revival was as much a revival of the Welsh language as it was of Welsh religion and at the end of the eighteenth century the language was still proudly used by nearly all the people in Wales. This Welsh speaking people, numbered at about half a million (the same sort of number as speak Welsh today), lived mostly in the rural areas. Industrial areas like Merthyr Tudfyl had begun their development but Wrexham had the largest market fair and was for sometime the largest centre of population in Wales with 8,000 inhabitants.

The Welsh also regained confidence in the use of the Welsh language in the arts. Edward Williams (Iolo Morganwg, 1747-1826) was a poet in both English and Welsh and used his antiquarian interests to revive the cult of the druids. He introduced the Gorsedd of Bards to the eisteddfod at Carmarthen in 1819 and helped re-establish the importance of the eisteddfod in Wales.

CHANGE IN THE NINETEENTH CENTURY

The newly enriched cultural life of Wales continued during the nineteenth century. There was new poetic activity—railwayman John Ceiriog Hughes (Ceirio, 1832-87) born at Llanarmon D.C. wrote 'some of the finest lyrics in the Welsh language on such themes as nature, love and patriotism' (*OCLW*), Welsh language newspapers were established, the Cymmrodorian in London brought Welshmen together to consider Welsh history, the Eisteddfodau developed the interest of ordinary Welsh-speaking people in popular culture and Daniel Owen (1836-95) the tailor from Mold wrote his novels depicting the contact between Welsh Methodism and the new industry in Wales.

While religion and the language remained at the heart of Welsh society during the nineteenth century, the industrial revolution and the inward migration of people from Ireland and England to work in the coalfields and ironworks changed the shape of that society, affecting both attendance at chapel and the use of the Welsh language.

By 1900 the population had grown to two million and most of it was by immigration into the traditional border lands of Wales, mainly into the valleys of south Wales. Merthyr and then Swansea and Cardiff became the big urban centres of Wales. The change also brought a new element into the country—a working class, soon to make up the non-Welsh speaking majority in Wales.

Social change also brought widespread unrest among the poor; in the rural areas it is remembered by the Rebecca Riots of south-west Wales in the early 1840s, and in the new towns and industrial areas by more general violence, particularly the Chartist riots of the 1830s and 40s. The Government responded in 1846 with a Commission, made up of English lawyers, to inquire into conditions in Wales. After receiving evidence, some of it from biased clergy of the established church, their report linked the unrest to ignorance, the cause of which, according to the Commissioners, was the use of the Welsh language and the non-conformist church.

The Commissioners recommended that the use of Welsh should be discouraged and, in what Eric Hobsbawm calls a typical nineteenth-century reaction from representatives of the major state in a multi-nation country, proposed that the Welsh language be allowed to disappear. Following the Report, the speaking of Welsh was banned in schools and the notorious Welsh Not tag was introduced as a punishment for children caught speaking Welsh. The Report claimed that Welsh nonconformity was intellectually confined and was serviced by working class people who were subject to severe limitations and that, until the Welsh language was replaced by English and state education was introduced, ignorance would continue.

This attack was seen as an outrage and as an attack on religion and language alike. The Report became known as *Brad y Llyfrau Gleision* —the Treason of the Blue Books, because the Welsh witnesses to the Commission were regarded as traitors to Wales. There was a reaction among the Welsh in support of education but damage had already been caused to a language under threat.

It is no surprise, therefore, that incomers to industrial areas did not want to become Welsh speaking or to encourage their children to learn the banned language. This was often the case even though they had married into old Welsh-speaking families and heard Welsh at home and might have worked alongside Welsh speakers who had also come into the industrial areas for work. The ban on speaking Welsh in schools was removed in 1888 but even in working class families where one or both parents spoke Welsh it was often considered a disadvantage for their children to speak it. For most of the workers and their families the language of both home and work had become a Welsh dialect of English.

THE TWENTIETH CENTURY

In 1900 about half the population in Wales was Welsh-speaking but since then there has been a further reduction in Welsh-speaking with a move westward of the linguistic border of Welsh-speaking Wales. This is the Fro Gymraeg (the Welsh language region) where more than 80% of the population remain Welsh-speaking and the language is used in most spheres of life. The decline in area of the Fro Gymraeg was mainly by movement from the east of Wales, because of the proximity of the English border, but the presence of English-speaking holiday makers and retired people around the coasts of Wales was to cause the linguistic boundary to move inward from the coast as well. During the latter half of this century, the Fro Gymraeg has become more and more limited to west Wales.

The pattern for most of this century in the highly-populated industrial areas of Wales has been that Welsh was spoken only by a minority but for some of them it became a passionate concern. Even for them the language had a limited domain mainly in the home and chapel. Commerce largely ignored Welsh and, where there was a mixed family background, big decisions about work and marriage increasingly came to be made in English.

By the middle of the twentieth century, it looked as though the Welsh language, important as it had been in forming the nation, was falling into such a minority condition that it would soon have little continuing effect on the life of the nation. The majority culture became working class urban and its linguistic vehicle was a special Welsh variety of the English language. It was increasingly influenced by American popular culture, especially with the impact of American films, so much so that some observers called the newly industrialised areas American Wales. The new Wales became aware of itself in the Welsh writing in English of writers like Dylan Thomas (1914-53) Gwyn Thomas (1913-81) and Idris Davies (1905-53). Unmistakably native Welsh, they represented the outlook of new industrial Wales and began to provide a new cultural base for Wales.

REVIVAL OF THE WELSH LANGUAGE

One of the Welsh writers in English, Emyr Humphries (b.1919), showed a move to the 'second phase of Anglo Welsh writing, a phase more patriotic and more concerned with the Welsh heritage' (*OCLW*) and reflected a growing reaction against centralisation in British society. At the same time, there has been a remarkable change in the attitude to the Welsh language; from an attitude of disinterestedness or hostility, there has been a move to a 'strong tide of support' (Professor Harold Carter) for the language among the non-Welsh language speakers. The government has responded to this movement by accepting symbolic bilingualism in adopting Welsh forms and traffic signs. More important, Welsh language policy in schools has changed and become more positive in the encouragement of the language.

Since the 1950s there has been a growth in the number of Welsh language schools and the Gittins Report in 1967 laid down the framework for a policy to make schools fully bilingual. Numerous Welsh language schools have been established so that by 1989-90 13.5% of all primary school children were being taught through the medium of Welsh. The use of Welsh in schools has been further improved by the inclusion of Welsh within the National Curriculum in all the schools of Wales; with a right to 'opt out' at key stage 4 in some schools near the Welsh/English border.

The bilingual policy is not a party issue and, according to Madgwick and Rowe, is seen by the government as a low-cost, marginal, low-benefit policy which is justified because of the popular support for the language. It is too early to decide whether it can change the relative position of the language in view of the constant movement of people in and out of Wales—during the inter-war years 500, 000 emigrated and 250, 000 moved in. The policy has, however, opened up a real opportunity for all children in Wales to share in the old language and the Welsh language schools are particularly strong in areas where children come from English-speaking homes. Freedom to choose has brought new life to the language and the support for the promotion of Welsh-language teaching has only been the subject of objection in Welsh-speaking rural areas where the element of choice seems absent and the increased emphasis on Welsh has meant that some monoglot English speakers feel disadvantaged.

As the policy rests upon the right to choose between schools and the medium of instruction, the choice might be deliberately made more attractive to an even larger group of parents in Wales by placing an emphasis upon the language skills that are achieved by learning a second language and the recognition that a child can more easily learn a third language than the second. It might well be sensible for all bilingual schools to include the teaching of an additional European language from primary school age and so give Welsh children the opportunity to build upon both their Welsh and European heritage.

The tide of support for the Welsh language has led to legislation for the equal status of the Welsh language—in the Welsh Language Act 1967 and the establishment of the Welsh Language Board under an act of 1992. The changes have received public backing so far and this is understood in most quarters to be essential to continued success.

The Welsh language has also been maintained by a continued literary tradition, with writers such as the poet Waldo Williams (1904-71) 'the twentieth century's most astonishingly original poet in the Welsh language' and Kate Roberts (1891-1985), sometime owner of Gwasg Gee Press, 'generally regarded as the twentieth century's most distinguished prose writer in Welsh' (*OCLW*). The National Eisteddfod has also been essential in maintaining the standards of the language particularly with the introduction of 'the all Welsh rule' in 1951 and, in support of the work of the schools, the Urdd Gobaith Cymru eisteddfodau provide a wider platform and experience of the eisteddfod and its traditions for children and young people.

It is not clear how much of a contribution to the development of the language has been made by activist groups such as the Welsh Language Society (Cymdeithas yr Iaith Gymraeg). While the Society has carried out research projects on issues like housing and the environment in Wales, it is better known for its campaigns of civil disobedience in support of the language, including protest in favour of bilingual signs and forms. They appear to have received unspoken backing in the Welsh-speaking society and, although obviously expressing a linguistic nationalism, they have not alienated people from their cause, as have the more militant and violent activities of groups like Meibion Glyndŵr.

Cymdeithas yr Iaith was formed after a radio lecture given in 1962 by Saunders Lewis on the destiny of the language. In his broadcast talk he identified television as 'the Chief Assassin of the Welsh language' and a campaign followed for a separate Welsh language TV programme. The need for the separate channel was accepted by the BBC in 1974 but delays in implementing the provision led to the threat by Gwynfor Evans in 1980 to fast to death. As a result a Welsh television station, S4C, which included Welsh language programmes at its core, was established in 1986 and has become a base for the patronage of the Welsh language and its writers and performers in the media. Its existence is widely respected by speakers of minority languages in other parts of the world and is seen as a successful example of subsidised minority media provision.

The majority of people in Wales welcomed the new channel, but it must be said that many did so because they did not wish to receive the Welsh language programmes on their sets and were glad to have them set apart on S4C. In addition some have expressed concern that the resources in support of S4C are greater than for the English language TV produced in Wales and that more provision should be made for the majority of Welsh people.

The main concern of the majority about the language may, however, be in relation to employment. Fluency in the Welsh language is not the test of being Welsh or belonging to Wales and it would be unacceptable discrimination in most parts of Wales to introduce a general Welsh language preference test for employment. The Welsh Language Board in preparing guidelines might consider the provision of a ratio for employment which will relate the minimum number of Welsh-speaking public employees to the extent that Welsh is at the time spoken in that area. In some countries where there is a minority language, protection is given by introducing into the public service such a quota preference, which generally depends upon the percentage of minority language speakers in the particular area. It is a difficult system to operate but is seen as fair to both the monoglot majority and the bilingually proficient minority. It can, however, obscure the real need to ensure employment of properly qualified people in a way which ensures fair opportunity for employment.

Progress in protecting the language, particularly in the schools policy, has a been a major achievement and goes beyond what is normally proposed for the protection of minority laguages. It is widely admired in other countries, although the British government still refuses to sign the European Charter of Minority and Regional Languages. The Welsh language is used by a significant minority in Wales as a means of communication and is entitled to protection as a minority right.

Welsh is also part of the Welsh heritage and this is appreciated by increasing numbers of the majority: for some non-Welsh speaking Welshmen interest in the language is a search for past roots and many want to encourage the extension of its use. It is, however, still a sensitive issue and progress in the bilingual policy depends upon the growing good will of the majority, the avoidance of compulsion and discrimination and the understanding that it is as important to express Welsh identity in the English language as it is in Welsh.

MODERN WALES

Among the historic foundations of identity in Wales, religion and language are still strong influences but alongside them there are more recently developed characteristics, some of which have grown out of them. The association of Welsh people with radical politics and sport are perhaps the most obvious examples from the history of modern Wales, but these are not the only features which may be seen as giving Wales its distinct character. As with religion and the language, exhibiting such features is not proof of Welshness, nor is it a test to pass in order to be considered Welsh. Many 'Welsh' characteristics are shared with other nations and regions with similar backgrounds so that they are not exclusively related to the national identity of Wales; they can often be found where there is a strong sense of belonging to the community.

Apart from the foundations, Wales has its symbols—like David, the Welsh patron saint, and the Welsh emblems of the leek, daffodil and the dragon to give further substance to the ideas about identity and nationality. In spite of the decline in the use of the Welsh language and

Welsh nonconformity there has been a new emphasis upon such symbols and emblems as a basis of identification with the country.

1. RADICAL POLITICS

One of the most observable of modern features of Welsh identity is to be found in the combination of national identity with social aspirations. Eric Hobsbawm said that 'the national feelings of the Welsh and Scots in the UK did not find their expression through specialist nationalist parties, but through the major UK opposition parties'. Since the beginnings of popular suffrage in 1867 there has been a tradition of radicalism in Welsh politics which arose out of the nonconformist strength of the nineteenth century. Until the Reform Act of 1867 most of Wales had had continuing Tory representation, often with parliamentary seats held for generations by members of the same landed family. But with the General Election of 1868 'the three hundred years reign of the squires came to an end' (Gwyn A. Willliams). The Liberals won 21 seats, the Conservatives only nine, and this Liberal supremacy remained until replaced by the rise of Labour Party representation in the 1920s. The high point of Liberal representation in parliament was in 1906 when not a single Tory M.P. was returned and the extent of the party's influence in Wales was reflected in Lloyd George's appointment as Prime Minister in 1916.

After World War I a Lib-Lab association came to an end and in 1922 the Labour Party gained 18 seats, Liberals 11 and Conservatives 6. From then on the electorate in Wales has returned Labour as the largest party and since 1945 Labour have received about 50% of the votes cast.

There have been variations in the general pattern—in 1966 Gwynfor Evans was elected as nationalist M.P. for Carmarthen and since then there has been a growth in nationalist representation. In 1979 and 1983 there were increases in Conservative representation, but by the 1992 General Election the pattern of earlier years had been clearly re-established: Labour 28 seats (49.5%), Cons 5, (28.6%) Plaid Cymru 4 (8.8%) Lib Dems 1 (12.4%). In the most recent European elections (1994) a similar voting pattern provided Labour with 58% of the total votes cast—all 5 seats returned Labour. The Welsh Nationalist Party moved into second place in the total of votes cast, with 17%, the Conservatives had 14% and the Liberal Democrats 8%. With the 1997 General Election, Labour further improved its parliamentery standing in Wales and for the first time since 1906 there were no Conservative MPs elected in Wales.

This solid radical voting pattern is also seen in the county council elections in Wales. The impression that party politics only arrived in local government with the rise of the Labour Party is incorrect. With the establishment of the County Councils by the Local Government Act 1888, the Liberal Party took power decisively in both north and south Wales. In Wales 'the new county councils showed more strikingly than in any other part of Britain the new transition to democracy' (K. O. Morgan) and their particular commitment to education gave the new Welsh communities their new county schools as a priority.

After World War I, the Labour Party also became important in Welsh Local Government, especially in south Wales, and many Liberals started to stand in local government elections as Independents. In the 1990 elections county council representation in Wales was Labour 288 (58%), Ind. 123 (24%), Cons 27 (5.4%), Liberals 22 (4.4%), Plaid Cymru 22 (4.4%), Others 12 (2.4%). The Labour Party was obviously the largest party, with over half the seats, but still did not have as big a proportion as the Liberals had had in the first county elections. In 1996 county councils, as the upper part of a two tier system, were replaced by single tier counties and county boroughs, and some of the very strongly Labour supporting counties like Gwent, Mid and West Glamorgan have disappeared, but the new political map looks remarkably similar—Lab 723 (56.8%), Ind 290 (22.7%), Plaid Cymru 113 (8.9%), Lib Dem 82 (6.4%), Cons 41 (3.25), Other 22 (1.7%).

POLICIES

The distinctive political position in Wales has been made clear in the political causes adopted by the ascendant parties. The Liberal periods in government reflected the importance given in Wales to mainly nonconformist issues like education, disestablishment of the Church of England in Wales, Sunday observance and teetotalism. The particular Welsh nonconformist agenda was a list of social and religious issues, so much so that when Disestablisment was finally introduced in 1920 it looked as though liberalism had achieved 'its historic objective', (K. O. Morgan).

There was little interest in separatism and devolutionary proposals were presented as a means of achieving the social and religious aims of Wales. There was a move among the Liberal leaders for home rule, but it was not a plan for separation. Gladstone, who had a family home in Hawarden in Flintshire, argued the case for Welsh Home Rule in a speech in Swansea that gave Welsh political nationalism its first encouragement. The cause was taken up by some Welsh Liberal M.P.s like Lloyd George who said in 1890 that Wales should have the same provision as that then proposed for Ireland and should 'no longer serve as the standard bearer for another nation'. Lloyd George was for quadrilateral home rule—for England as well as Wales, Scotland and Ireland and he made the relief of congestion in parliamentary business the main reason for the proposals. The proposals did not have the general support of Welsh Liberals and Home Rule was not achieved. The constitutional consequence of legislation on Welsh issues was, however, the start of the process of decentralisation of Government.

For the Welsh people at the beginning of the twentieth century, industrial activity based upon the coal and steel industries had created a new economic and political world and South Wales became the growth area of Great Britain. The booming industrialisation brought new political opportunities to the urbanised people of Wales and it resulted in the growth of the Labour Party. During the early years of the Labour Party 'South Wales was the capital of British Labour' (K. O. Morgan). The Welsh nonconformist tradition was an important element in the Labour outlook and it was, for instance, clearly present in the miners' leader, William Abraham (Mabon 1842-1922), who represented the mixture of chapel, work and politics. He was elected M.P for the Rhondda in 1885 and presented his politics as 'based on the simple truths of the New Testament.' Mabon was first elected with Liberal support as part of the Lib-Lab alliance but in 1906 Labour became a separate party and the nonconformist link placed Welsh Labour in a good position to become the successor to the Welsh Liberal cause. This tradition was sustained over the years by James Griffiths (1890-1975), architect of the welfare state and first Secretary of State for Wales and more recently by later Labour Secretaries of State for Wales, such as George Thomas, a President of the Methodist Conference.

The early proposals, pre-World War I, of the newly formed Labour

Party saw devolution as the way of building the economy fairly and improving the lives of the working class. Kier Hardie (1856-1915), the first Labour M.P. member for Merthyr from 1900 and Leader of the Labour Parliamentary group until his death, advocated the cause of local democracy. His socialism emerged from the local culture and was the basis of policy based on local democracy, decentralisation and accountability.

In 1918 the Labour Party conference voted for an assembly for both Scotland and Wales but, as the economic depression of the twenties arrived and worsened, the priority changed. In order to meet the needs of Wales and other disadvantaged regions a policy of economic centralism was adopted. This approach matched the mood of the country and reflected a view in Labour which was different from that of Mabon and Kier Hardie and tensions within the Labour Party in Wales reflected those in the country as a whole

The alternative force within the Labour Party came from the materialist, sometimes Marxist, view of people such as Noah Ablett (1883-1935). Ablett, like many others in South Wales including James Griffiths, had been affected by the 1904 Evan Roberts Pentecostal Revival but, unlike Griffiths, Ablett became a Marxist. He succeeded Mabon as leader of the Miners' Federation and campaigned for revolution and workers' takeover of industry in the form of workers' syndicalism. In this materialist tradition was the leadership provided by Aneurin Bevan (1897-1960). Like other similar radicals he broke with the forms of nonconformity and local community government and advocated central planning solutions to the problems of inequality and deprivation. For Bevan and many other south Wales leaders, 'Welsh patriotism appeared irrelevant and the obsession of a minority', (Gwyn A. Williams) and was a distraction from the cause of solidarity of workers throughout the UK. This was the general view adopted by the Labour Party in the inter war years and was reflected in their policy during the period after World War II when it had a large parliamentary majority. The priority then was to develop the national welfare state and use central planning as a means of equitable redistribution of wealth.

Although the difference of approach was fundamental within Wales and the Labour Party as a whole, none of the Welsh Labour protagonists of devolution, when the issue was raised, were separatists and, as will be seen later, their arguments for devolution were mainly set in a regional context and within the Union of the United Kingdom. This was the position of the former Labour leader and Welsh M.P. Neil Kinnock, who gave the Labour commitment to an Assembly for Wales and a Parliament for Scotland. This integrationist approach is part of the present policy and while some of the old arguments against devolution are still heard informally, the Labour Party policy has returned to the Mabon-Hardie vision of democracy for the people of Wales.

Liberal and Labour politics have both been important in the formation of modern Wales and have helped sustain a Welsh identity based on radical politics. Although they have not taken a nationalist position and, for most of the periods in which the parties were in government, did not legislate for more devolution than was necessary to give effect to other policies, both Liberal and Labour have kept the economic and social needs of Wales as an important and distinct part of their central government programmes. During the twentieth century neither the Conservative Party nor Plaid Cymru (since its formation in 1925) has received majority support in Wales but, as will be seen, the Conservatives have fashioned Welsh institutions of government and Plaid Cymru, as the nationalist party, has presented a challenge to the programmes of the other parties in Wales. Party support has for many Welshmen been the expression of their particular national identity.

PEACE MOVEMENT

Outside party politics, the force of Welsh radicalism may be seen in the peace movement in Wales. Since 1868 when Congregational minister and Liberal, Henry Richard, was elected M.P. for Merthyr, the peace movement has been part of the Welsh political scene. One of the first M.P.s to present the Welsh nonconformist views in parliament, Richard was known in Westminster as the M.P. for Wales. He was a supporter of the Charter movement and stood for parliament on the basis of 'Wales and the Working man' Opposed to jingoism, he pleaded the cause of disarmament in and out of parliament and became known as the Apostle of Peace for his work in support of arbitration and world solidarity.

Richard's example has been followed by action for peace. The

Temple of Peace was built in Cathays Park in Cardiff; in 1934/5 a National Peace ballot organised by the League of Nations showed that the highest returns were obtained in 12 Welsh constituencies; Urdd Gobaith Cymru's international message of goodwill became an annual peace activity and the establishment of the International Eisteddfod in Llangollen was seen as a mark of reconciliation after World War II. When the Campaign for Nuclear Free Zones received extensive support as part of the Campaign for Nuclear Disarmament in the seventies, each of the eight Welsh counties passed resolutions of support and gave some indication of the underlying support for peace action. The protest campaign aginst American missiles was started with a march from Cardiff and for some time in the eighties, the CND movement acquired 'more weight and spirit in the valleys and elsewhere in Wales than any merely political body', (Gwyn A. Williams).

Although the Peace Movement has not been a single party cause in Wales, those who joined have been able to look to the radical background of Wales for support and have themselves contributed to the identity of Wales.

2. Sport in Wales

Sport in Wales, especially rugby football, came to evoke a keenness which sometimes seems to be a passion replacing religion and politics. Through its national teams, it has brought many to cheer for Wales who might otherwise have rejected any idea of sharing in Welsh identity.

National support for football started in north-east Wales with Welsh soccer and the establishing of the Welsh FA at a meeting at the Wynstay Arms, Ruabon in 1876. At that time the game was still being formed and there had not been any clear separation of soccer and rugby (the dribblers and the handlers) and the Wrexham F.C. could field, as they did in 1873, fifteen players. At first called the Cambrian Football Association, the name Football Association of Wales was adopted before the first international against Scotland in 1876. There was a Welsh cup played for by seventeen teams in 1877/78 and won by Wrexham with a team made up of people from the area—mainly miners and shopkeepers. The north-east was the centre for Welsh soccer and provided many of the Welsh players. A teacher at Chirk, T.E. Thomas, was a noted enthusiast and through his efforts over twenty Chirk men played for Wales in the first 25 years of Welsh soccer!

Soccer remained relatively unknown in South Wales until the 1920s when Cardiff City became the leading club, fully professional and winning the F.A. Cup in 1927. International games have made Association Football important in providing a representative side for Wales. The first overseas international in 1933 against France ended in a draw; in the World Cup in 1958, Wales defeated Israel in the first round, but lost to Brazil in the quarter finals. In the 1960s it was agreed that the winners of the Welsh cup could take part in the European Cup winners Cup and Wales has taken its place alongside other European countries in competition. Like rugby, Association football provides the opportunity to cheer for the national side as well as participate locally.

While Welsh soccer has been and remains important, it is rugby that for many represents the sporting life of Wales. Although preempted by soccer in north Wales, a national organisation for rugby, the Welsh Rugby Football Union, was set up in 1881 and the first international against England was played in that year. The game provided a formidable way of bringing into the community the large numbers of people moving into south Wales at the time. The population of Wales increased by a million between 1871 and 1911 and most were concentrated in south Wales. In 1914 one magazine said that rugby had discovered a democracy which acts as participant and patron. As was said in Smith and Williams' centenary book of the WRU, *Fields of Praise*, 'It was where doctor and lawyer could ruck happily shoulder to shoulder with miner'.

Although rugby is now seen as a proper reflection of the nation's spirit, there was at first a great conflict between the chapels and the new game. Ministers preached against participation, partly because many of the local clubs were linked to public houses, and the conflict came to a head in the 1904 Evan Roberts revival when its preachers singled out rugby to be attacked. The impact of that Revival was great and it looked as if the chapel might have at last made contact with the new industrial masses. In Ynysybwl the entire team was converted and baptized and all sporting activity ceased there for three years. In Kenfig Hill, Jenkin Thomas is quoted as saying 'I used to play full back for the Devil, but now I'm forward for God'. (Quoted by Smith & Williams).

The conflict concealed the affinity between the community religion and the new community sport and the common background of the chapel and rugby supporters. After the 1905 match with the All Blacks, one New Zealander said the atmosphere gave 'a semi-religious solemnity to this memorable contest', (again quoted by Smith and Williams) and it was in that year that a colliery clerk from Llantwit Fadre wrote the tune for 'Cwm Rhondda' and brought the hymn singing imagery of the chapel into the playing field with new force and enthusiasm.

In its formative years rugby did not gain ground in north Wales, with soccer firmly entrenched and looking to Merseyside for its premier soccer clubs. It was not until 1931 that the North Wales Rugby Union was formed and, although both codes are now a distinct part of the national scene, the north still maintains a different emphasis in its support for soccer.

Both games have had to provide rules in order to answer the question of Welsh identity but not to answer the test as to which team one should shout for. While identification with the national team is a real expression of belonging to a country and Welsh teams have enjoyed the backing of people in Wales, it was also important to establish the qualification to play for the country. Here the rules have had to be formulated and do not depend upon whether the individual concerned feels Welsh or not;in the absence of any statutory basis for Welsh nationality, they at least provide one objective test of being Welsh.

For the first years of both rugby and soccer, the rules about qualifying were loose but have now been agreed, although they are not the same for both games. They are as set out in the table, together with the qualifying rules of Welsh Athletics, another well-supported national sport in Wales.

RUGBY	SOCCER	ATHLETICS.
Born in Wales	Born in Wales.	Born in Wales
Welsh parents	A Welsh parent.	A Welsh parent.
Welsh grandparent.	Welsh grandparents.	
Resident in Wales for at least six years.	Born outside UK and holding British passport.	Resident in Wales for at least 2 years.

The three main sources of nationality—place of birth, parentage and residence are to be found in various forms as alternatives. If any of

55

these 'qualifications for Welshness' listed were adopted generally, it would make for many more Welshmen living outside Wales than in the country itself and they give some indication of what could be involved if there were legal tests of Welsh nationality. As it is now, support for a national team depends on the sense of belonging and is a good test of being Welsh. It is an area where no matter what the differences between Welshmen, they firmly consider themselves Welsh. Welsh sport provides for both players and supporters an awareness of being Welsh and it holds this in common with the other foundations, characteristics and symbols of nationality.

3. *SYMBOLS OF NATIONALITY*

Wales is not short of the symbols of nationality. Wales has a Patron Saint, David (d. 589) or Dewi, who lived in Wales in the heroic age and was famous for his simple life. There are a number of miracle stories told about David, such as the formation of a new hill at Llanddewibrefi so that people could see and hear him preach. Since at least the twelfth century he has been a focus of national pride for Welshmen, especially for those who associate Wales with religion, peace and spirituality.

David is sometimes associated with another of the famous Welsh symbols—the emblem of the leek, and is there associated with the fighting side of Welsh life. David is said to have ordered the Celtic soldiers to wear a leek on their helmets in battle against the pagans and the leek is still worn as a badge cap by the Welch Regiment. Since the annexation in 1284, Welsh soldiers have played an important part in support of the armies of the Crown. 'The long bow was more of a Welsh than English weapon', (Coupland) and at Crecy in the mid-fourteenth century, one third of the English army consisted of Welsh archers and spearmen. The Welsh regiments formed since then include the Welsh Guards, the Royal Welch Fusiliers, recently celebrating its tercentenary, and the Royal regiment of Wales (formed in 1969 by an amalgamation of the Welch Regiment and the South Wales Borderers) and all have played their part in forming people's symbolic understanding of Welsh identity.

In the nineteenth century the daffodil became a popular emblem of Wales and was a favourite of Lloyd George. Although the origin of the use of the daffodil seems to depend upon the similarity of the name with that of the leek (*cennin* for leeks, *Cennin Pedr* for daffodils), both are used to mark Welsh identity, especially on March 1st, St. David's Day.

There is also the Welsh national flag which shows the red dragon, heraldic symbol of Wales, on the green and white background and this is also said to go back to the heroic age of old Britain when, according to tradition it was associated with King Arthur. It was on the flag of Cadwaladr (d.664) whom Henry VII claimed as his ancestor. Henry carried the Red Dragon into battle at Bosworth in 1485 and the Tudors adopted it as part of the royal coat of arms.

The national anthem of Wales, *Mae Hen Wlad fy Nhadau*, is a product of Victorian times. It was written by Evan James of Pontypridd and his son James in 1856 and became popular as the national anthem of Wales when adopted by the rugby crowds at the beginning of this century. In 1955 Cardiff was designated as the capital city and with its magnificent civic centre, it has become both the national and regional centre of Wales. The identification and acceptance of both a national anthem and a capital city play a part in creating the sense of sharing in a modern nation.

Is there also a royal symbol for Wales by the continuing use by the monarch's eldest son of the title of Prince of Wales? It was adopted at the end of the thirteenth century as a sign of English conquest and there is no evidence that the subsequent succession of Princes of Wales have regarded themselves as having any particular constitutional identification with Wales. There have, however, been some ceremonial associations with Wales—Henry VII named his first son Arthur in association with the ancient King and in this century the Princes of Wales have been invested at Caernarfon Castle. Both these investitures were promoted by Welshmen, Lloyd George in 1911 and George Thomas in 1969, and added to the Welsh symbols in the presentation of the heir to the British throne to the people of Wales. The description of Wales as a Principality is still quite common and, although there is a view that the idea of an 'English' Prince of Wales should be rejected as a mark of subordination, there appears as much support for British royalty in Wales as in most parts of the UK. If there is a future for the British monarchy, one development might be for the Prince of Wales to have a residence in Wales, with a special role within the Principality. At least the heir to the throne will not be troubled by being the Head of the Established Church in Wales.

Foundations, characteristics and symbols are all significant for Wales. Those considered here for Wales do not provide a comprehensive and exclusive list for there are others with which people in Wales may identify, such as singing and acting and particular food and dress. Neither do they provide a test which must be passed in order to be considered Welsh but they do go towards making for identification by 'a sufficiently large body who regard themselves as members of a nation' (Hobsbawm).

References and further reading.

H.Carter, 'Patterns of Language and Culture 1961-1990', 1990, *Cymmrodorian Society Transactions*.

Church in Wales, *Wales in Europe: Core or Periphery*, 1992.

Corrigan, *100 Years of Welsh Soccer*, 1976, Welsh Brewers.

R. Coupland, *Welsh and Scottish Nationalism*, 1954, Collins.

R.R. Davies, *History of Wales (1063-1415)*, 1987, Clarendon.

E.J. Hobsbawm, *Nations and Nationalism since 1870*, 1992, Cambridge.

Geraint Jenkins, *Protestant Dissenters in Wales*, 1992, University of Wales.

G.Lloyd Jones, 'Welsh in schools', 1991, *Cymmrodorian Society Transactions*.

J. Lloyd, *History of Wales—to Edwardian Conquest*, 1912, Longman.

Madgwick and Rowe, *Territorial Dimension in UK politics*, 1982, Macmillan.

K.O. Morgan, *Labour People*, 1987, Oxford.

K.O. Morgan, *History of Wales—Rebirth of a Nation*, 1981, Oxford.

F. Muir, *The Frank Muir Book*, Heinemann, 1976.

Prys Morgan, *Welsh Society and Nationhood*, 1984, University of Wales.

Alwyn Roberts, 'Some political implications of S4C', 1989, *Cymmrodorion Society Transactions*.

P.R. Roberts, 'Welsh language, English law and Tudor legislation', 1989, *Cymmrodrion Society Transactions*.

D. Smith & G. Williams, *Fields of Praise*, 1981, University of Wales.

M. Stephens, *Oxford Companion to the Literature of Wales*, 1986, Oxford.

George Thomas, *My Wales*, 1986, Century.

Glanmor Williams, *History of Wales (1415-1642)*, 1987, Clarendon.

Gwyn Williams, *When was Wales?*, 1985, Penguin.

W.R. Williams, *History of Great Sessions in Wales*, 1899, Brecon.

Chapter 3

NATIONALITY AND SOVEREIGNTY: WALES IN BRITAIN

In looking at the strands that have made Wales a nation, there is the further element that in time past Wales had its form of separate sovereignty and exclusiveness in the form of government. Although this was before modern ideas of sovereignty were developed, it was important to Wales at the time and is still a distinguishing feature of Wales's historic identity. In this chapter the history of sovereignty in Wales is outlined, followed by a brief consideration of the way concepts of sovereignty, affecting Wales as part of the United Kingdom, have developed. It is interesting that the idea of the sovereignty of the Queen in Parliament, which is the result of these developments, now appears inadequate to meet the constitutional needs of either the people of Wales or those in other parts of the UK, and slowly a national (UK) constitutional review is taking place.

THE HISTORIC SOVEREIGNTY OF WALES AS A NATION

For years before the accession of the Tudors and the passing of the Act of Union (1536-43), the Welsh claimed sovereignty for themselves. The claim was asserted in the Middle Ages by poets and princes—'the sovereignty of Britain (*unbeniaeth Prydain*)' was a ritual warcry and Owain Gwynedd (d1170) staked his claim to be the 'true proprietor of Britain' (R.R. Davies). This sort of aspiration was 'the staple political ideology of mediaeval Welshmen' at a time when Wales still saw itself as the 'sole inheritor and guardian of Celtic influence'. These were, however, pleas for past glories to return and related to a larger country than the land of Wales itself; aspirations rather than declarations of the position in the country.

The picture of Wales as a land of warring tribes, which was the position up to the time of the Edwardian Conquest in the late thirteenth century and was reflected in Giraldus Cambrensis' comment that the Welsh refused 'to submit to one ruler' (quoted by R.R. Davies), makes it necessary to approach the search for the past sovereignty of Wales with some caution. It is, however, reasonable to argue for the existence of such a past sovereignty, at least to the extent that it will mark out Wales as a historic nation.

The Laws of Wales made for a community which, though divided into tribes for most of the time of independence, exercised over the whole of Wales the vital political activity of law-giving and observance. The bards of Wales provided unity in the culture; the Welsh Laws provided a unity in a legal framework for the whole of Wales. There was a subordination to the Laws of Wales throughout the country and, even if at any particular time there was no Prince of all Wales, the whole of Wales accepted the Laws. As some modern Federal states accept their Constitution as binding on Federal and State governments alike, so the princes applied the laws whether they ruled the tribes of Gwynedd, Powys, Deheubarth, Gwent, Morgannwg or one of the lesser kingdoms. The laws of Wales gave clear authority to the king, prince or leader, and it was from the laws that such authority came. It was 'the cement of society, the bulwark against social chaos. He who will not give right (or law) has no place in a country, as the ancient Welsh aphorism has it', (R.R. Davies).

Apart from the unity under the Law, it is also possible to maintain that for many years, from the rule of Rhodri Mawr in the nineth century, a single authority was exercised over the whole of Wales by the High Kings of Wales. They were the Welsh leaders strong enough to command the allegiance of the other princes and while there were limitations on their exercise of power—generally treaty obligations and the exception of parts of Wales from their rule—there was enough authority to regard even warring Wales as a nation.

When the Roman Empire broke up in the fourth century, the imperial power was handed over by Magnus Maximus (Macsen Wledig) to the Romano-British notables. Macsen was a Roman soldier from Galicia, probably speaking a kindred Celtic language to that of the Britons and he is said to have married Helen, a daughter of one of the families of Gwynedd. Gwyn A. Williams considered that Wales was born in AD383 when Macsen made his transfer of authority to the princes or chiefs of the tribes. These princes lived by warfare and conquest, fighting each other, as well as the alien.

The dynasties established from Rhodri Mawr (d.878) remained the most powerful until the death of Llywelyn II (Llywelyn ein Llyw Olaf) in 1282. Rhodri was the first of the High Kings and from his base in Gwynedd won control of much of Wales. It was his family that was to provide the dynasties of both Gwynedd in the north and Deheubarth in the south west. While the tribes split up on Rhodri's death, his grandson, Hywel Dda (920-950), who ruled Deheubarth, reclaimed the land held by his grandfather as King of all Wales, except Brycheiniog and Morgannwg and was proclaimed 'By the grace of God ruler of all Wales'. He was the first Welsh king to strike coins bearing his title, Hywel Rex, and his authority was so powerful and good that, apparently following the precedent of Alfred the Great in England, he was able to call the parliament or assembly at Whitland in Carmarthenshire to approve the Codification of the Welsh Laws.

Some ninety years of strife followed Hywel's death. Gruffudd ap Llywelyn (d.1063), 'offspring of a strategic marriage into the southern branch of the Rhodri dynasty' then took power in Gwynedd in 1039 and held the whole country during the last years of his life and almost to the date of the Norman invasion. To the Anglo Saxon chronicler, Gruffudd was the king 'over the whole of Wales' who hounded the Pagans (Vikings) and Saxons in many battles, (R.R. Davies).

After the Norman invasion, another from the Rhodri dynasty, Owain Gwynedd (d.1170), adopted the title 'prince of the Welsh' and was called by others 'king of Wales' (R.R. Davies). The territory for which Owain Gwynedd could claim any sort of sovereignty was, however, limited but the record of expansion of Gwynedd under Owain shows that he paid little regard to the distinction between Welsh and Anglo-Norman neighbours. (R.R. Davies). Owain Gwynedd's grandson Llywelyn ab Iorwerth (d.1240), called Llywelyn I or Llywelyn the Great, set out to re-unite both Native Wales and 'the Welshies' of the Marches. By 1215 he had taken virtually the whole of Wales. He presided over the Council of the Princes of Wales, gave aid to King John and the barons and even obtained protection for Welsh Laws and liberties in the Magna Carta. He negotiated with King John at Worcester in 1218, married the daughter of the king and from 1218 until his death in 1240 was king of at least native Wales.

After the death of Llywelyn I, it was his grandson, Llywelyn ap Gruffydd, Llywelyn II (Llywelyn ein Llyw Olaf, d.1282) who next claimed, by victory in 1258, the title Prince of Wales. This was confirmed in the Treaty of Montgomery made with the English king Henry III in 1267 and many of Llywelyn's territorial gains in the Marches were accepted, although some annual tribute to the English crown was also called for. Llywelyn II was the first Prince of Wales to be legally recognised by the English. Except for Owain Glyndŵr, he was also the last Prince of Wales to exercise anything like real sovereignty over Wales.

The nature of the sovereignty exercised by Rhodri Mawr, Hywel Dda or any of the other High Kings of Wales is difficult to describe. Their rule was long before modern constitutional concepts were worked out, although the position was probably not very different from elsewhere in Europe at the time. If, however, past sovereignty is some test of present nationality then Wales should qualify both because of the rule of the Kings and, especially, because of the unity of the Laws.

The Edwardian conquest which followed the death of Llywelyn in 1282 is considered the real conquest of Wales by an outside power. The Statute of Wales or Rhuddlan of Edward I (1284) claimed subordination of the whole of Wales in these terms—'Divine providence hath now of its favour wholly and entirely transferred under our dominion the land of Wales with its inhabitants' and the Native Wales was included in the structure of English local government. The title 'Prince of Wales' was given to the eldest son of the King of England and references to the Principality appear. The process of subordination and loss of separate sovereignty was almost complete.

It was, however, still possible for the King of England to recognise Welsh civil law, rights and customs—the Welsh Laws—among the native Welsh, subject to the rights of the settlers to use English law and the acceptance of subordination to the Crown. In Marcher Wales it was different and more independent of the King, because the mixed feudal society continued with little control, and as a result maintained its own leadership which, sometimes, as in the case of Owain Glyndŵr, was to seek support for revolt in the whole of Wales.

The rebellion led by Owain Glyndŵr showed that the Norman conquest had not ended the claims in Wales to be an independent country. During the century that had followed the conquest in 1283, there had been several rebellions among people in Wales, but the final claim to independence came from Owain at the beginning of the fifteenth century. His action combined discontent with the Norman conquest with a peasant revolt against economic suffering and the aftermath of the Black Death and what began as an isolated uprising by a Marcher Welsh lord became a national cause.

Owain Glyndŵr was related to the Anglesey branch of the ancient Tudor family, had been trained in the English court and according to Gwyn A. Williams was the 'complete Marcher gentleman'. His main properties were at Carrog in the Dee Valley and at Sycharth (Chirklands) in the Tanat Valley. A dispute with Lord Grey of Ruthin, and an inability to get justice in the King's court, led him in 1400 to attack Ruthin and other towns in north-east Wales. The vindictive English response was the immediate cause of his campaign for Welsh independence. He received support from his family connections (his Tudor cousins, Gwilym and Rhys, captured Conwy Castle for the Owain Glyndŵr cause in 1401) and from other powerful leaders in Wales; he also received widespread popular support throughout Wales, including that of ecclesiastics, gentry and peasants. He presented an agenda which would have created a new Wales and a new relationship with England. He called on the old war cries against the 'mortal foes the Saxons', and acquired 'the basic paraphernalia of princely power', (R.R. Davies) which included making alliances with foreign countries: he entered into a treaty with the French and sought support from Robert III of Scotland. By 1404 Owain had control of nearly all parts of Wales and called a parliament in Machynlleth and another, with representatives from each commote or district in Wales, in Harlech in 1405 to legitimise his success. He proclaimed himself Prince of Wales and presented a programme which included the establishment in Wales of two universities and the creation of a new Welsh church with its own metropolitan archbishop at St. David's. In the end, however, 'he simply did not have the resources to sustain a national revolt' and the harsh winter of 1407-8 'proved the final blow', (R.R. Davies). The process of reconquest by the English was slow but was concluded after the accession of Henry V in 1413 when there followed a period of punitive repression. Owain Glyndŵr's movement for independence was the final attempt at creating a separate government for Wales and the course of Welsh history in the century that followed the rebellion showed that Wales's future lay in union with England.

Another Tudor, Owain ap Meredudd (d. 1461), had been taken on by Henry V as a page boy and later married his widow and through the marriage of his son Edmund to Margaret Beaufort (d. 1509) the Tudors became protagonists on the Lancastrian side in the War of the Roses.

At the end of the fifteenth century, the victory of Henry VII, grandson of Owain Tudor, brought revived hopes of the reconquest of Old Britain. In fact, as has been seen, it brought deliverance from oppression as the Tudors in their successful new dynasty gave recognition to Welsh support and involvement, with relief from the earlier penal laws, opportunities for Welshmen in the London court and participation in the the administration of Wales—but no reconquest.

Constitutionally, the accession of the Tudors seems to have brought legitimation to the Edwardian annexation of Wales and the acceptance by the Welsh and English of the Anglo-Celtic state. The cultural identity of Wales survived but from this time any issues of sovereignty and the rights of the people of Wales become legally bound to the common history of both England and Wales—an Act of 1746 even provided that statutory reference to England should also include Wales.

THE BEGINNINGS OF PARLIAMENTARY SOVEREIGNTY

When the Tudors established Britain—England and Wales—as a formidable nation state, they appealed for support to the people as a whole—both English and Welsh. Public goodwill was increasingly seen to be necessary to the Crown, partly because of the importance of a popular national identity and partly because the people's leaders and representatives held the purse strings for much of the time. The feudal nobility were replaced by an official elite based upon merit and within this elite were a number of important Tudor supporters from Wales. As a result of the Act of Union, the number of Welsh supporters in London was increased by the M.P.s elected from the new Welsh counties and these London Welsh were to help create a new imperial Britain. New national myths acknowledged Celtic origins and Arthur and the ancient Kings of Britain were appropriated by the new nation state. When the church became Protestant it, too, looked to its roots beyond the Anglo-Saxon or Norman invasions and the Celtic church and its saints were taken as the origin for a separate national church.

While Parliament became more important under the Tudors, the sovereign power in the nation was still based upon a personal authority of the monarch and it was this claim to authority that became the source of bitter conflict under successors to the Tudors in the seventeenth century. The new Stuart Kings were Scottish kings who had acceded to the English throne on the death of Elizabeth and, in a way similar to the Tudors, claimed to rule as monarchs by divine right. Unlike the Tudors, they were not able to maintain the support of parliament and in this dispute, which led to the Civil War and the execution of Charles 1, the courtiers and the group supporting the king still firmly included the London Welsh.

Although they had originally gone to London to help the Welsh Tudors, the leaders of Wales remained loyal to the royalist cause under the Stuarts. During the Civil War, they supported the King against parliament's challenge to royal absolutism. There were some exceptions which were to point the way to a radical cause in Wales and these included the dissenting preachers like Morgan Llwyd and Vavasor Powell. The landed gentry of Wales, however, led Wales in opposition to the Parliamentary armies and in resistance to Puritan evangelization.

After the Restoration of the monarchy in 1660, the fortunes of the court party returned and even though the Stuart kings after the Restoration were Catholic in religion, the High Tory landowners remained loyal. In the persecution against Dissenters that followed, the leading supporters of the government, including Judge Jeffreys of Acton, Wrexham, played a prominent part. The leaders of Wales only reluctantly accepted the 'Glorious Revolution' which brought James II's reign to an end and firmly shifted sovereignty to the Crown in Parliament.

The new ideas of sovereignty at the end of the seventeenth century meant that the country, which under the Tudors had been the first to become a nation state, became the first to rationalise the process of government on a democratic basis. The political philosophers argued for a contract between society and the ruler which gave the government power to rule. Thomas Hobbes in 1651 in his book *Leviathan* had laid the foundation for the doctrine and argued that 'the contract' was voluntary, but having been made was irrevocable and indivisible. Hobbes's concepts were developed and related to the supremacy of parliament and the beginnings of parliamentary democracy in 1689 by John Locke in support of the Glorious Revolution and the replacement of James II by William and Mary.

Locke's argument was that the surrender of the people's natural rights to their rulers was limited to those necessary for the common good, that the legislature was sovereign among governmental powers, that the executive acted on its behalf and that the king remained only as the formal sovereign. The people who had entered into the contract were the political society and political sovereignty was vested in them, although, unlike the King, Parliament and Executive or government, they were not given institutional form. As Charles Merriman points out in his *History of the Theory of Sovereignty*, the contract was not an historical fact but an idea based on the declaration that every just law is to be made as if the contract were its foundation. It reflected, however, the revolutionary change in the view about sovereign power in England and Wales in the seventeenth century and gave the basis for a constitutional monarchy. It was also to influence the later developments in America and other countries sharing in British history. It seems relevant, too, in contemporary consideration of proposals for devolution in the UK.

SCOTLAND AND THE UNION

The concept that Parliament was sovereign provided the setting for the Act of Union 1707. Although the Crowns of Scotland and England had been united with the accession of the Stuarts, it was seen as essential that for the creation of a united country the parliaments of the two countries should unite. Unlike the Tudors, who had managed through the Crown to unite England and Wales into a common and shared system, their Stuart successors were not similarly able to bring uniformity to England and Scotland. Scotland had maintained a separate church and laws and, for part of the time, a separate parliament. The Act of Union 1707 united the two parliaments, and gave a united sovereignty in the Westminster parliament. In return Scotland was able to share in the common prosperity of the two countries and the other pillars of the Scottish nation—the Kirk and the

Laws—were recognised and protected. The Act of Union 1707 also confirmed agreement to the Hanoverian succession to the Crown, and the Kingdoms of England and Scotland were to be united in the kingdom by the name of Great Britain with a flag combining the crosses of St. George and St. Andrew. (With the addition of the cross of St. Patrick in 1800, it was to become the present flag—the Union Jack).

AMERICAN APPLICATION OF THE CONCEPT OF POPULAR SOVEREIGNTY

The proprietorial attitude of the British government towards America and its British colonists and the expectation that they should be taxed without representation led in the late eighteenth century to conflict and the American War of Independence. 'The English traditions were ignored by an obstinate king and his second rate advisers' (Coupland) and revolution followed. The ideas behind the revolution and the process of establishing democratic control in America were, however, as Liah Greenfield says in her *Nationalism—Five Roads to Modernity*, 'a direct continuation of the process begun in England in the sixteenth century'.

The colonists developed the social contract concept of Locke that all power resides in the people by declaring that their sovereignty should be formally vested in them by a Constitution. It is this written constitution which gives Americans their declared inalienable rights, protects their liberties and gives American government a theoretical basis for power and responsibility to be shared between the Federal Government and the States.

Many of the Welsh Dissenters had moved to the communities in the American colonies for freedom to worship freely and, like their predecessors in Wales in the seventeenth century, were prominent in the revolutionary movement: 18 of the 56 who signed the Declaration of Independence are said to have been of Welsh descent. At home in Britain the eighteenth century saw the growth of radical support among new Welsh intellectuals and some of the members of the new county societies in Wales became, in Gwyn A. Williams' phrase, 'spiritual Americans' and strong supporters of the colonists in their struggle for constitutional change and freedom from absolutism.

At the beginning of the nineteenth century, British national leaders were frightened by the prospects of revolution and the ideas of the social contract. Its concepts were seen to have been a basis for the American War of Independence. In France, Rousseau developed the doctrine of the social contract to justify revolution if the rights of the community were not vested in a democratically chosen body and the slogans of the French revolution of Liberty, Fraternity and Equality seemed to come directly from such ideas. As a result the British concepts of sovereignty and the nature of political power did not move towards the American concept of inalienable rights for the people in a Constitution. Instead British jurisprudence moved into a narrower mould of positive law based upon the teaching of John Austin and A.V. Dicey .

John Austin, whose main work on Jurisprudence appeared in 1832, agreed with Hobbes and Locke that the king in parliament was sovereign and that nothing, legally speaking, was impossible for parliament to do. He also argued that legal theory should be limited to concern with the precise consideration of the legislative will of parliament and that positive law, which limits interpretation to the actual words of the laws, was the only subject for constitutional study. It seemed to follow that if the laws were the command of the king in parliament they should not be subordinate to the people's rights in a written constitution nor to the judiciary in enforcing such rights.

It also seemed to follow from this theory of law that there was no scope for a sharing of responsibility between Westminster government and other levels of government. Any organisations for administration established under the law were subordinate to Parliament and could be abolished under the laws. Austin had provided a materialist base for law and government and, in doing so, shaped the particular British nineteenth-century view of sovereignty.

The theory of the 'absolute, infallible, indivisible and inalienable' will of parliament was refined later in the century by A.V. Dicey. He drew a distinction between absolute legal sovereignty of the Queen in Parliament and the political sovereignty of the electors but this political sovereignty legally stood outside the realms of positive law and was not given any institutional form such as a Bill of Rights or a Constitution. Dicey's restatement had reinforced Austin's position in

British law schools, especially as Dicey's view on more detailed constitutional matters was very influential.

The view of sovereignty which claims uncontrolled power for the British Parliament is still considered 'a peculiar feature of the British Constitution' which exerts 'a constant and powerful influence' (Professor E. W. Wade), even though it has been overtaken by such legal events as joining the European Union and by contemporary constitutional and political needs, such as the need for power sharing within the UK itself. The general need for a basis for sharing sovereignty is suggested by the definition of the state as the community coming together for the purposes of government and points to the desirability of a constitutional provision which would meet the needs of levels of government both below the nation state, like Wales, and levels above the state like the European Union.

SHOULD SOVEREIGNTY BE SHARED?

The propositions about the unqualified power of the State and Parliament have rested on nineteenth-century theoretical considerations which were a British response to the needs of the time. As has been seen, after the War of Independence the Americans, with an outlook shared with the British on fundamental matters like freedom and representation, moved forward with alternative theoretical views. The absolutist view of law has become increasingly isolated, the exclusive concept of sovereignty more irrelevant and there is no reason to be tied into such a position.

The absolutist view of the law and government has not been without its critics in Britain and the need for some limitation of the view has been pointed out by leading lawyers and theologians. Lord Denning, for instance, held the view that the protection of the individual depends upon 'the instinct for justice'and 'the traditions of liberty' applied by the courts. This suggests a basis for government which is not exclusively determined by the letter of each parliamentary law and Lord Denning quoted the seventeenth-century lawyer Coke, the Lord Chief Justice of his day, who told James I, 'The king is under God and the Law', and claimed that this epitomised in one sentence the great contribution made by the common lawyers of England. Denning emphasises that whoever is ruler is under the law and suggests that in Britain, too, there are obligations of freedom and justice to which Parliament should conform.

Theologians have also argued for recognition that the state has no ultimate and omnipotent authority of its own. The Catholic Church has long had its tradition of recognising the divine law of justice as the basis for a jurisprudential system and in a series of lectures in Scotland, a continental Protestant theologian, Professor E. Brunner drew on these ideas to argue for a more structured society in which the nation state plays a part, but where liberty depends on institutions of community built up of layers from the locality. He pointed to the totalitarian dangers of reliance upon a theory of positive law and argued for proper regard for custom and tradition; a view shared by the nineteenth-century constitutional lawyer, Maine, who wrote about the need to take account of the custom and practice of a community in the application of the law by the courts. A modern constitutional historian, Victor Bogdanov has taken the same theme in his definition of a democracy as 'the exercise in power by the people influenced by history' and views on the necessary limitations on sovereignty appear in a 1996 ecumenical publication in Wales: 'Any tendencies to absolutism should be resisted. The danger signals are present, and an alarm has been sounded about the "elective dictatorship" and the highly centralised state in which we live' (*Wales: A Moral Society?*).

If a limit is to be placed on absolute power in Britain and there is to be a protection of individual freedom and a protected partnership of power, there needs to be constitutional change. Constitutional lawyer Professor Wade agrees that the power of the government is excessive and believes control has passed into the hands of the executive. He considers that there should be a written constitution which the judges should uphold on oath.

A former Master of the Rolls Sir T. Bingham, has also attacked the absence of an institution to provide constraint on the unrestricted power of parliament. Too much power is placed in the executive, especially the Prime Minister, without proper checks and too much detail is put before parliament with insufficient time to deal with matters of law reform. The sovereignty of the people becomes the principle of the 'sovereignty of the state' which, once created democratically, is all powerful. The need for constitutional reform was highlighted by Lord Hailsham in the Dimbleby Lectures in 1976. He also described the present position as no less than 'an elective dictatorship' and, while he praised the British constitution for its immemorial antiquity, claimed the powers of our Parliament are absolute and unlimited. It can take away a man's liberty or life, prolong its own life as a parliament and increase the powers of government. Lord Hailsham supported the case for constitutional reform to protect the individual and community and proposed a Bill of Rights with devolution all round to provide for a proper sharing of powers in the UK.

TERRITORY AND PARLIAMENTARY SOVEREIGNTY

Apart from any defect arising from the unlimited powers of parliament, the traditional view of sovereignty has proved inadequate in defining jurisdiction. One of the elements in the positivist view of law and government is that the exclusive rights of a nation state are related to a particular territory and that the territory defines a jurisdiction which is not subject to any external authority. This gave the legitimation of authority over people at home and gave the right and duty to defend the homeland. When overseas territories were acquired, it was thought appropriate to apply the doctrine there too and so justify the defence of the acquired possessions against other colonial powers.

The weaknesses of the doctrine became apparent when proposals were made for the constitutional transfer of power to the colonies. Independence for the colonies brought transfers of sovereignty by Acts of Parliament which provided for the end of sovereignty even though the doctrine of parliamentary sovereignty prevents parliament from binding its successors. The fact that most of these newly liberated nations adopted the old colonial boundaries did not change the constitutional defeat of the doctrine of sovereignty—in the Statute of Westminster in 1931 British sovereignty was clearly limited because Section 2(ii) of the Statute specifically provided that no law of the Dominions should be void or inoperative on the ground that it was repugnant to English law, whether present or future. This was a fundamental change in which the limitation of sovereignty of parliament was accepted by parliament itself.

The weakness and potential dangers in the doctrine of sovereignty being vested in parliament are also seen in the limitations it placed on action to deal with home rule in Ireland. Before 1914 the nationalism of the minority nations in the United Kingdom had had a low profile and until 1922 the almost unchallenged sole political unit for the four home countries of England, Scotland, Ireland and Wales was the United Kingdom of Great Britain and Ireland. Until that time change might have taken place in Ireland within a United Kingdom, but the opportunity was lost. By 1931 Ireland had become a republic and Northern Ireland had been granted devolved powers. The history of relations between Ireland and the rest of the United Kindom shows that the British doctrine was as inadequate to the needs of the home country as it was in dealing with external territories. It must surely have contributed to the record of instability and hostility between Ireland and the UK.

Ireland had nominally been a province of England since the eleventh century and effectively so since the fifteenth century. The Act of Union with Ireland was the last of those provided within the UK and was not passed by Parliament until 1800. The Union Act provided a separate judicature and a separate administration for Ireland under a Secretary of State for Ireland, but made no provision for a parliament with legislative powers. Ireland had representation at Westminster and was clearly made subject to Westminster sovereignty like the rest of the country.

Claims by the Irish for devolved Home Rule in the later nineteenth century were presented at Westminster but they were rejected, mainly because of the opposition of the Unionists in the north and support in the UK for the union based upon the indivisible sovereignty of the Westminster parliament. The claims for devolution were replaced by those for independence and independence for Southern Ireland came after revolution. In 1922 the Westminster Government of Ireland Act formally gave dominion status to southern Ireland similar to that given to former colonies of the United Kingdom and the claimed sovereignty of the United Kingdom was broken to become the United Kingdom of Great Britain and Northern Ireland. Whether a different course would have resulted from a concept of sovereignty more like that adopted in America is speculation, but George V is quoted as saying to Ramsay

MacDonald in 1930 that if Britain had accepted Gladstone's Home Rule Bill, the problems of the Irish Free State could have been avoided.

The Government of Ireland Act 1922 provided for a Governor, a separate Parliament and Government for Northern Ireland and they were given powers under the Act in relation to domestic matters. There was all the appearance of a federal sharing between the Province with its devolved powers and the centre at Westminster, which retained imperial matters like defence and reserved matters like taxation. The 1922 Act was, however, a statute which made no proper provision to settle disputes between the central government and Northern Ireland and had no constitutional recognition of the rights of the people of Northern Ireland. Westminster chose to act as if there were federal arrangements without providing a proper constitutional basis. It refused to take account of complaints about prejudice in housing allocation and changes in the election system to the disadvantage of the minority. As was shown later the powers were only devolved and in the absence of an adequate constitutional theory of sharing of sovereignty the Northern Ireland parliament was legally subordinate to Westminster. When it came to the test in 1972 the Northern Ireland parliament at Stormont could and did have its powers withdrawn.

At least part of the reason for the inability to find a satisfactory constitutional settlement for the North of Ireland must be the inadequate view of British governments on sovereignty and the hope for a more peaceful Ireland still depends on overcoming some of the prejudices created by old ideas of the Union. The proposal for no further change in the Union without majority consent in the Province creates the possibility of a new approach and is a necessary safeguard but again makes nonsense of the government views on sovereignty in the United Kingdom. It is assumed that sovereignty can be given up and the Union broken if there is a majority at the time of the vote in favour of separation in the Province and makes such an assumption without a proper constitution by which to make a binding legal statement of the status of the Province. It remains to be seen whether any satisfactory solution for Northern Ireland within the Union can be found without some such constitutional provision.

In Ireland the failure to provide an adequate solution to the limitation of sovereignty may have led to the separation of Southern Ireland and in doing so triggered off a nationalist response that led to the setting up of another separate and exclusive state.

In the nineteenth century there had been widespread support in Europe for the Liberal alliance of nationalism with democracy and Mazzini developed in Italy the popular concept and slogan 'one nation, one state'. This view of nationalism asserted that the nation is the correct organisational unit for government and was applied in the settlement after World War I, with the historic existence as a former sovereign state taken as a test for meeting claims for independence. The test of former statehood was however, applied selectively at the will of the victorious allies. There were moreover difficulties in justifying the new status on this basis and an artificial population limit of 2½ million had to be introduced to make the doctrines work in practice. While Wales had the necessary population, the possibility of applying the doctrine to Wales never arose. It was a doctrine that rationalised the war settlement, and the position in Wales was not then an issue.

In the period since the World War I settlement, nationalism has been tainted by its association with the rise of fascism and then, after the defeat of the Nazi powers, by the division of Europe. The West followed the path of integration by starting to share sovereignty in the European Community and in the East the Russian hegemony subordinated most of the nations created after World War I. Since the break up of Communist domination, old nationalisms have reappeared with new claims for separate sovereignty. In some of them, the inadequacy of nationalist solutions of exclusivism has become terribly apparent.

The former British Foreign Secretary, Lord Howe, said to a United Nations meeting in Mold in 1994 that he hoped the European Union would be able to tame nationalism without destroying the sense of political identity and economic unity, which he describes as patriotism. This concern with the dangers of nationalism and the link with separate sovereignty have led to support for an enhanced role for the region within Europe. Some speakers in Wales have used the term nationalism in a way that would not involve separate sovereignty—

thus the then Archbishop of Wales, the late Dr G.O. Williams wrote 'there is a place for the kind of nationalism that seeks to secure for Wales whatever degree of autonomy is needed to control vital decisions affecting the life of the nation' (quoted in *Wales, a Moral Society?*). This is far from advocating a separate state and is consistent with the view that by sharing sovereignty within Britain and Europe, there is the prospect of nations and regions being able to express their identity in a way that reflects the needs of the modern society.

SOVEREIGNTY IN A GLOBAL COMMUNITY

The idea of exclusive sovereignty vested in the nation state is not only a poor constitutional framework for the United Kingdom; it is also outmoded as a way of determining relations between nation states generally. One practical justification for exclusive sovereignty of the nation state has been that it should provide a basis to protect trade and industry and encourage enterprise in its own national way. Historically such protection has been considered important to the great mercantile nations like Britain but the needs of effective international relations have now changed. The growth of communications, the international economy and the needs of the environment make the protection of the nation state increasingly less relevant. Commerce and trade use the new communications technology to deal internationally and information can move instantly from one place to another without reference to nationally controlled economies and their boundaries. The world markets increasingly follow and depend on money flows rather than upon goods and services protected by national systems. Transnational companies have their vital research and development in any country that suits them and they produce where the economics of manufacture dictate. C. W. Jenks, in his *Law in the World Community*, considers that the national economies which the nation state once protected are no longer capable of such protection.

The limited value of territorial protection by the nation state are also seen in the need for international care of the environment. The consequences of the Chernobyl nuclear accident in 1986 are still felt in the sheep-rearing areas of Wales and Cumbria because the ecological consequences of human activity are not limited by national boundaries and transnational ecology protection is needed to control pollution and save natural resources. There are other examples of the need for global order, such as the world-wide nature of crime and terrorism. For solutions to be enforceable on this scale there is need for a jurisdiction which is wider than that of the nation state.

In many matters of global concern, the nation state is already being matched by other units for making policy decisions and undertaking enforcement. The supra-national groups like the European Union (see Chapter 4) provide a response in legal and institutional terms to the changed needs of society and the economy. The Union depends upon a concept of government that replaces exclusive sovereignty of the state but is itself limited by geography in its jurisdiction. In some of the other areas of international concern, there is a need to develop a truly global system which would give adequate expression to the needs for world trade, the protection of the environment and the prevention of international crime. The UN provides the basis for such a system but it needs to become more effective and to relate global action to a foundation of common values, based upon the acceptance of human rights in a common law of mankind (Jenks).

The nation state may have declined in importance but it remains significant for its history and for the operation of functions that are not so international that they are better dealt with at a supranational level and are not so regional or local that they would be more appropriately dealt with at a lower level. The nation state may thus remain important but it will depend upon a recognition that sovereignty is now in decline and the need is to move away from claims by the nation state for absolute powers to a more adequate view of government based on a community coming together for the range of functions and purposes for which they are best suited. It is equally important for stateless nations and regions to see that a search after exclusive sovereignty is inadequate, irrelevant and dangerous and that in the proper context they might expect to serve their communities as regions or nation regions sharing government with the nation state and the supranational body.

References and further reading.

T. Bingham, *European Convention of Human Rights*, 1990.

V. Bogdanor, 'Europe, Subsidiarity and the British Constitution', *RSA Journal*, April 1994.

E. Brunner, *Justice and the Social Order*, 1947, Lutterworth.

E. Chappell, *Wake up, Wales*, 1940.

R. Coupland, *Welsh and Scottish Nationalism*, 1954, Collins.

Cytun: Churches Together in Wales, *Wales:a Moral Society?*, 1996, Cytun.

R. R. Davies, *History of Wales (1063-1415)*, 1987, Clarendon.

Lord Denning, *The Changing Law*,. 1953, Stevens.

P. Drucker, *The New Realities*, 1989, Heineman.

L. Greenfield, *Nationalism—Five Roads to Modernity*, 1992, Havard.

Lord Hailsham, *Dimbleby Lecture*, 1976, BBC.

E. Hobsbawm, *Nations and Nationalism since 1780*, 1990, Canto.

J. Lloyd, *History of Wales—to Edwardian Conquest*, 1912, Longman.

C. W. Jenks, *Law in the World Community*, 1967, Longman.

Madgwick and Rowe, *Territorial Dimension in UK Politics*, 1982, Macmillan.

C. E. Merriman, *History of the Theory of Sovereignty*, 1900, Colombia.

H. Miall, (ed), *Minority Rights*, 1994, Pruler

J. L. Parker, *Salmon on Jurisprudence*, 1937, Sweet & Maxwell.

Writson and Grunwald, 'Twilight of Sovereignty', *RSA Journal*, September 1992.

E. W. Wade, *Administrative Law*, 1988, Oxford.

Gwyn A. Williams,. *When was Wales?*, 1985, Penguin.

Chapter 4

WALES IN EUROPE

The place of Wales in Europe may now be looked at from the perspective of a nation region in Europe by considering first, in the context of Europe, the end of the nation-state and the limitation of old ideas of sovereignty; next the importance of Europe in promoting the region as an essential level of government; then the contribution the regions have so far made to Europe in regional networks, and finally the European recognition of minority rights.

EUROPE AND THE END OF THE NATION STATE

The European Union was established because important decisions could no longer be made at national level. When first established each of its predecessor organisations (the European Coal and Steel Community, Euraton, and EEC) was in the nature of an international body with each nation-state delegating decision-making. As the European activities have extended in range so the Union has become more like a supra national power and the trend seems to be towards a fully accountable constitutional union of states—this is reflected in the change of institutional names from European Communities to European Community to European Union.

Historically the Union developed out of the Coal and Steel Community, which was created in the early 1950s without British membership. The Common Market was a further development in order to aid trade as the Marshall Plan brought in American aid to reconstruction. Britain belatedly applied to join in 1961 but was rejected, mainly as a result of French opposition. After re-application, Britain was admitted in 1972 and this was confirmed by a referendum in Britain in 1976. With later admissions, of which Austria, Sweden and Finland in January 1995 are the most recent, there are fifteen member states, with a population over 350 million. The Union has developed an important regional policy and although the period of greatest growth had probably passed by the time Britain joined, the market created and supported by the Union has become vital for British industry and over half the total British exports are to other European Union countries.

Economic need may have been the main reason for the formation of the market, but there have been other aims as well. One was the need to unite Western Europe in a constitutional collaboration to prevent a resurgence of militarism in Germany and to face the threat of the Cold War. The role played by the North Atlantic Treaty Organisation has, however, overshadowed the part played by the European Union in defence. This was obvious at the time of the failure of the Union to provide an adequate response to the difficulties in Yugoslavia and Europe was said, at the time, to be economically a giant, politically a pygmy but militarily a mouse!

Another aim of the Union has been to improve the social environment for a diverse society to flourish in an economically united continent. This reason has become more important with the collapse of communism and the removal of fears of military attack from the Warsaw powers. Some of these countries are now seeking to join the European institutions and the idea of the 'common European home' has become a new base for European solidarity.

THE COMMON EUROPEAN HOME

The common European home is based on shared values and a common heritage on which have been built separate national cultures and is separate from the importance of the European Union to the economy of the different countries. Its heritage rests on a cultural history that includes the Middle Ages, the Renaissance and the Enlightenment. Although marred by frequent wars, this shared culture has the Christian religion at its core. Professor W. Pannenburg of Munich University says, 'It would be difficult to conceive of modern European culture without its Christian background and heritage'. Even the divisions of traditions into Orthodox, Roman Catholic and Protestant took place within a Christian Europe though of course the differences are reflected in the particular cultures where they are dominant.

The common cultural heritage is given formal support and recognition by the European Union in article 128 of the Treaty of European Union (the Maastricht Treaty) which acknowledges the diversity of cultures within a common framework. It provides that 'the Community shall contribute to the flowering of the cultures of the Member States, while respecting their national and regional diversity and at the same time bringing the common cultural heritage to the fore.'

Apart from such 'statutory' encouragement from the European Union for cultural growth, another European institution, namely the Council of Europe, of which Britain was a founder member, has played a vital part in identifying the connections in European culture and has encouraged a number of independent organisations, like the European Centre for Traditional and Regional Cultures (ECTARC) in Llangollen, to assist in this work.

Within the Christian Churches of Europe, there are bodies concerned to promote unity in action in Europe. Among them are the Catholic Conference of European Bishops, the Conference of European Churches and the wider and more informal ecumenical movement, such as the young people's ecumenical gatherings at Taize in France. They provide a contemporary Christian foundation for ethics and motivation in the Union and give a representation of a common European point of view. At a Cathedral service in St Asaph to mark the start of a county Europe week in 1988, Jean Fischer, secretary of the Conference of European Churches said that the Conference repres-ented a fellowship of 120 member churches from all over Europe. It had been formed after World War II to support reconciliation and the firm conviction 'that there cannot be and must not be another war, that Christians should refuse the division of Europe into blocks, and there should be peace among the churches.'

WALES AS PART OF THE COMMON EUROPEAN HOME

The interaction between the common European heritage and that of the different nations within Europe can be seen in ancient nations like Wales, where the Welsh cultural history has been fundamentally influenced both by its position in the United Kingdom and by its place in Europe. For example, the roots of Welsh culture are to be found in the Celtic tribes that spread across Central and Western Europe. These tribes established in the Czech Republic, Slovakia, Hungary, Austria, Switzerland and South Germany a culture based upon iron-working and horse-riding and, in the Halstatt culture of the sixth century B.C., established the 'fine flower' of the iron age. These Celts, or Gauls as the Romans called them, spread beyond this central area and are now best remembered by their surviving cultures in Brittany, Cornwall, Wales, Ireland and Scotland. Each of these regions has a special part to play in the presentation of the ancient history of Europe, none more so than Wales where the Celtic language is still a common language.

The Christian Church has helped maintain the European influence in Wales from the Age of the Saints in the so called Dark Ages and, although reluctant to accept the authority of Rome, the Celtic Church in Wales has, at least since the time of St Garmon (Germanus) followed the Western European Christian tradition. It was, however, with the coming of the Normans that Wales became fully a part of European cultural life. The Normans brought, in particular, a new way of church life that was directly based on that which was in existence elsewhere in Europe. The new church and monastery buildings and the new orders of priests and monks altered the cultural life of Wales. Scholars working in the monastries provided translations of the older Welsh legends and history, such as the stories of Arthur, to give a base for a new European tradition of chivalry and romance. This tradition, in its turn, influenced new poetry in Wales, and Wales became part of the community of Europe and has remained there.

The Reformation put Luther and Calvin among the spiritual heroes of Welsh Protestantism and after Tudor times the Welsh people, especially the landed elite of Wales, were able to share in the British-European developments of thought and art. The history of Wales and its language, religion, culture, radical politics and sport are part of its identity as a separate nation-region, but do not stand in isolation. They are a part of both British and European history. John Osmond in *Welsh Europeans* senses an increasing identification of Welsh people with Europe and says, 'Yet since the 1950s history has been driving Welsh people away from Britishness and towards a new duality in which belonging to Wales is felt more and more in conjunction with a sense of belonging to Europe'. Whether this change in emphasis is right or not, the Welsh heritage is both British and European and Wales shares in a British and European identity.

While the heritage of Europe provides a bond between the separate nations of Europe, it is the constitutional creation of the nation states that has made Britain subject to the same legal authority as the other members of the European Union (EU). The limits on the value of the British doctrine of absolute parliamentary sovereignty, which have been discussed in the previous chapter, have been apparent for a some time. The public awareness of this inadequacy has grown as Britain has moved closer to Europe. The attitude in Wales to the Westminster government and sovereignty has changed and the authority now vested in the European Union makes the concept of constitutional power-sharing more familiar. This change in attitudes has been described as one of the main reasons why people can find the idea of constitutional change within the UK more acceptable than when the referendum on devolution took place in 1979, (J. Barry Jones in A *Parliament for Wales*).

THE EFFECT OF MEMBERSHIP OF THE EUROPEAN UNION

The legal effect of British membership of the EU is that sovereignty is now shared between Britain and the other member nation states and the European Institutions. Unlike the statutes recognising the independence of the British dominions and colonies, the British legislation dealing with the entry of Britain into Europe recognises that legal authority in respect of British citizens is now partly vested in the European Union. The European Communities Act 1972 provided for the recognition of Community Law, and Section 2(i) of the Act applies such recognition to existing and to future Community Law. Community Law determines whether a particular provision is directly effective, and the national courts, sometimes with the help of the European Court of Justice, interpret and apply the Community Law.

The concept of international law in some European legal systems gives straightforward recognition of the supremacy of international treaties, but some in Britain, influenced by the old ideas of the absolute sovereignty of the British Parliament, argue that transfer of power under an international treaty is only a delegation and that, by implication, the entry into membership has also been a delegation by Britain to the European Union. It is also argued that parliament could not be bound by earlier legislation, but both arguments overlook the fundamental nature of the change brought about in 1972: Parliament ceased to be sovereign because 'this was one of the inescapable conditions of membership' (Professor E. W. Wade).

The implications of a shared authority between the Community and the nation state have, so far as Britain is concerned, been recognised by the British courts. In a case called Factortame in 1990 a Spanish fishing claim was referred by the House of Lords to the European Court and its decision was accepted, conceding that European Law applied even though there was a contrary domestic British Law. The European Court, which was set up under Community Law, adjudicates on matters of community law and also applies general principles, similar to English common law. The decisions are enforced in national courts but the European Court considers this to be an exercise of European sovereignty in the matters referred to it. The Court considers, therefore, that the transfer under the Act has involved more than the delegation to the Union of the right to legislate and that consequently a directly effective provision of Community Law prevails over a provision of national law, at least as long as the nation state remains a member of the Union.

While the European Communities Act gives the force of law to existing Community legislation and provides for future Community Law to have direct effect in Britain, any Community Legislation must be approved by the Council of Ministers, which includes a British government minister. This gives the national government considerable control and the position of the British parliament is also protected by the scrutiny reserve which provides for a debate to be held if demanded by a select committee of Parliament, although for such a review to be more than a formality would require a new contact system between the various institutions, including the British MEPs, Westminster MPs and possibly for the future representatives of a regional assembly or parliament. These practical issues have to be resolved in the future but do not obscure the constitutional change which brings citizens of Britain within a European jurisdiction. Europeans now have a shared law, as well as a shared history.

The Convention on Human Rights was established as early as 1950 and was one of the first major collaborative acts in Europe after World War II as a Treaty between the members of the Council of Europe. Britain played a major part in drafting the Convention and duly ratified it but has not yet directly incorporated it in British statute. The implications of the Convention for British sovereignty have arisen because of the support given for the Convention in the British courts. In one law case in 1974 it was said that in interpreting British legislation, it was, 'hardly credible that Parliament would act contrary to the Convention'. Lord Denning made a similar point in a 1975 case in which he said that the courts could and should interpret acts of parliament so as to conform with the Convention. In a more recent case concerning Derbyshire County Council the British Court of Appeal referred to provisions in the Convention in deciding the legal point that a local authority could not sue in libel.

The British courts have almost reached the point of making the European Convention part of English Common Law and there is an expectation that if there should be a British legal provision that infringes the Convention, Parliament will change the law. The former Master of the Rolls, Sir T. Bingham has said that a 'central function of modern democracy is to protect human rights' and it is in recognition of this that the Human Rights Convention, administered by the Council of Europe through a Commission and a Court in Strasbourg, has become a vital part of European Institutions. Because the British government has so far been unwilling to incorporate the Convention into a British act of parliament, either by a specific provision or within a general Bill of Human Rights, there are a relatively large number of British claimants, who having been unsuccessful in finding a common law remedy, have to make use of the remedies available under the European Convention.

EUROPE AND REGIONALISM

SUBSIDIARITY AND THE VOICE OF THE REGIONS

While the movement to decentralise and deconcentrate the activities of the state by the sharing of powers was not started by the move to

European integration, the regionalist movement has undoubtedly been strengthened by it. Increased centralisation by the transfer of some presently state-controlled powers to a supra government has led to the growth of a counter-balancing emphasis on the diversity of communities and cultures within Europe.

The European Union's response has been to recognise this and to promote the idea of an equilibrium between the Community, the member state and the region. It has promoted the doctrine of subsidiarity which would ensure that actions and decisions should take place at the lowest level which is appropriate. While the European Union philosophy is that some functions are better carried out at a larger than state level, it follows as a corollary that certain 'other governmental functions might best be exercised at a level smaller than that of a member state' (V. Bogdanor).

While the European institutions have taken this positive view as general policy, the reference to subsidiarity in the Maastricht Treaty only relates to Europe and the member state. Article 3b provides:

> In areas which do not fall within its exclusive competence, the Community shall take action, in accordance with the principles of subsidiarity, only if and so far as the objectives of the proposed action cannot be sufficiently achieved by the member state.

The British government saw the clause as support for the national goverment as the member state but the German representatives saw it as an opportunity to reaffirm the constitutional importance of the regional level, because in Germany the reference to the member state clearly includes the Länder (German regions) as well as the Federal Government. Regions within unitary and centralised states like Britain are not given specific acknowledgement in this clause and, although benefiting from the Treaty by the creation by the Union of a Committee of the Regions, they will have to await future revision of the clause to give proper effect to the subsidiarity doctrine.

Although at the present time it may not be constitutionally possible for the regions to be given authority directly under the Treaty, the status of the regions has been given a great deal of support by the European Union. The President of the Commission at the time of the Maastricht Treaty, Jacques Delors, spoke of the future of Europe as being in 'its peoples, states and regions'. The European institutions support regionalism, both by encouraging the recognition of their regions' status within the member states and by emphasising that it is possible to be both cosmopolitan in outlook and rooted in the region and locality.

The arguments for the recognition of the role of the regions have also been supported by the Council of Europe. In its report on Culture and the Regions, and in the ten-year study that preceded it, the Council concluded that

a) the regions' cultural impact should be to encourage rootedness and identification with the local area and provide a balance between centralised and local cultures, and this was incorporated in the European Declaration on Cultural Objectives in 1985.

b) Economically the region should be the base for economic development either by direct provision or by co-operation between the business world and the public. 'The . . . market integration in Europe seems to favour a higher profile for the regions in establishing their own strategy to attract investment, people and partnership', (E. Delgado in introducing the report).

c) The region can bring pressure on central government on important issues and provide a strategic framework within which the local authorities can operate. It can set planning and environmental guidelines and provide for democratic and human rights within the region in a way which balances state provision and control and

d) however limited the powers of a region might be, it can help the state to concentrate on its own responsibilties at national and international level.

These conclusions are modest but provide a useful basis of action for the regions of Europe, even those whose powers are not so limited as these conclusions envisage.

In such a European setting, the overlapping identities in Europe of belonging to the state, region and locality are welcomed as part of the equilibrium between the different identities. These identities may be characterised by a common history, geography and social and economic bonds and the pursuit of common interests of the sort described above in relation to Wales as a nation region. Some regions will be other than a nation-region. They may be states within a federal system, others may be regions with an identity as strong as that of the nation-regions and yet others may be without a pre-existing sense of regional identity. The Council of Europe view is that a region which has no strong cultural characteristics can nevertheless build an identity for itself by a determination to achieve economic and social objectives, and this practical approach gives the widest basis for making the region a common element within the European constitutional structure.

EUROPEAN INSTITUTIONS IN SUPPORT OF THE REGIONS

The growth of support for regions as representative units of government has been helped by the institutions created by both the European Union and the Council of Europe.

In 1988 the Consultative Council of Local and Regional Authorities was established by the European Union's Regional Development Directorate to liaise with the European Commission and the Commission directorates on regional affairs, and, as mentioned below, Wales was represented on this Consultative Council through its representative on the Assembly of European Regions. The regions were given further recognition under article 198 of the Maastricht Treaty which replaces the Consultative Council with a formal Committee of the Regions. The article provides for the consultation of the Committee by the Council of Ministers and the Commission, and for the Committee to issue opinions on its own initiative: it makes the Regions of Europe a direct and active constitutional part of the European structures. It should now be possible for the Committee to argue for powers for the regions within the member states.

The European recognition of the regions and the appointment under article 198 of representatives from the regions has highlighted a weakness in the British position where the selection is made by central government. While the composition of the Welsh membership is from local authority representatives, the nomination is made by the political parties to central government, and even this was a concession made by Westminster after pressure and opposition to a proposal for the Welsh Office to represent Wales directly. There are now three Welsh representatives on the Committee and they have started their work on the various topic committees, such as rural planning, regional policy, transport and social affairs.

The European Parliament has also supported the recognition of the regions and has backed calls for the provision of a Council of the Regions which would act as a second chamber of the parliament. The case for a second chamber of the regions might properly form part of an agenda for another review of the Maastricht Treaty.

The Council of Europe has also supported the development of institutions for the regions. In 1957 it appointed a Consultative Committee of Local Authorities and Regions (CLARE) followed in 1994 with specific provision for a Chamber for Regions in a Congress of Regional and Local Authorities in Europe. The Congress, which has over two hundred members from 32 countries, is seen as the 'third pillar' of the Council of Europe—the others are the Committee of Ministers and the Parliamentary Assembly, made up of representatives of national governments and parliaments repectively. The Council of Europe has developed many of the regionalist principles which are commonly accepted and, through its committees, prepared the Charters of Minority and Regional Languages and of Local Self Government (although neither of these Charters has been adopted by the British Government). The Council is currently considering a draft Charter of Regional Autonomy which should cover what support should be given to regions in unitary countries where the position of the region is not adequately recognised. It will deal with the important relationship of the region to the locality so that help might be given to local authorities where the regional authority itself does not implement the subsidiarity principle.

As Wales is regarded as a region in Europe and there is recognition of its position as a historic nation, there is a European Commission office in Wales—the others are in London, Edinburgh and Belfast. The primary function has been to provide information about the European institutions and the office has provided for Wales a known European senior official as an unofficial ambassador to Wales.

REGIONALISATION BY EUROPE—FUNDING FOR THE REGIONS

Another way in which the European Commission has influenced the growth of regional importance, especially in the those areas and regions such as Wales that are seen to be economically disadvantaged, has been the use of the region as a unit on which to base a programme of economic and social cohesion. While the European Union's main funding is still in support of agriculture through its Common Agriculture Policy (CAP), the policy of providing economic help through the European Regional Development Fund (ERDF) for regions in need of support has become an important part of the European Union and makes up 25% of the budget.

The regional policy, which is now related to more funds than those provided by ERDF alone, is based upon a partnership between the region, state and the EU. The programmes are based upon regional development plans, involving, in Wales, the Welsh office and the local authorities. Because of the way in which the British government has administered the regional policy in Britain, it has meant that central government, which in Wales is the Welsh Office, has maintained direction over the allocation of monies and the Welsh Office has accordingly established a European division to manage the partnership and the preparation of the Welsh Regional Plan.

The EU principle most directly affected by British government direction of funds is that of *additionality*, which means that European monies are intended to supplement and not replace national programmes. The way the British government has interpreted this led to a dispute between the Community and regional representatives on the one hand and the British government on the other. Britain insisted that local authority projects should not be approved unless they were already in a capital programme approved by the British government. The response to this was that capital approval should have been enough to authorise funding without European assistance, and if not, the British infrastructure programme itself was being funded through Europe as a substitute for British funds. At one point money for the conversion of resources in the coal closure areas—the RECHAR Fund—was withheld for this reason. Whether by way of supplement or substitute, however, European funds have been vital in the provision of resources for regional economic survival from 1979 onwards.

Later changes in the rules for funding Regional Funds have emphasised the need for social and economic cohesion because it was clear that two areas in Europe which do not receive regional support have continued to attract the concentration of economic development. One is the Golden Triangle: London, Paris, Amsterdam and extending into the Ruhr Basin; the other is the area in southern Europe which includes S. Germany, N. Italy, S. France and Catalonia and Valencia in Spain. Changes in the funding system have put an emphasis on integrating the budgets in support of the disadvantaged regions. Four structural funds were identified—European Social Fund, European Agricultural Guidance and Guarantee Fund and the Financial Instrument for Fisheries Guidance, as well as ERDF—although ERDF still retains half the funding for projects. The Commission has also determined five regional objectives in the distribution of structural funds and for Wales this provides support for much of the region, either under Objective 2—areas undergoing industrial decline, or Objective 5b—fragile, rural areas undergoing social change.

Since the inception of the ERDF Wales has received £540 million in ERDF grants for specific projects for those parts of Wales currently qualifying under Objective 2. This funding has been to help the economic conversion of industries in decline and there is currently a £143 million programme over a three year period. Objective 5b is to help with the promotion of agricultural areas which are disadvantaged and provide economic diversification of fragile, rural areas. It, too, has benefited Wales directly with designated areas in most of Wales. It is expected that there will be a development programme of £140 million for the period 1994-99.

Wales has been a major beneficiary from Europe because of its low level of Gross Domestic Product, low level of incomes and high level of unemployment. Within the region there are areas which are from time to time excluded from support and they suffer disproportionately because of their proximity to favoured areas so that it would make sense for the whole of Wales to be treated as a unit for regional help, rather than rely upon areas determined by the British Government's travel-to-work areas.

The relevance of the regions is fundamental to the Commission: the policy document *Europe 2000* includes a Community Plan which covers transport, environment and other headings of European policies within which the regions as well as the member states may work, and the social and economic plans for competitiveness and cohesion are based on the development of the regions. The European Union recognises that because of factors such as inadequate basic infrastructure, levels of training, research and development and the limitations of local financial markets, there are some regions in Europe which are are disadvantaged within the member state and within Europe. Such problems hinder economic development and the building of Europe so E.U. policy places the region in the forefront of programme provision. It is of increasing relevance to all regions and particularly to a region like Wales which has yet to see improvement in its relative position on the economic league tables.

REGIONAL NETWORKS

THE CONTRIBUTION OF WALES AS A EUROPEAN REGION

The regional structures in Europe have included those created by the regions themselves. Through their elected representatives, they have formed or taken part in a network of committees and groupings that have affected the progress of European integration. This has had its impact in Wales on attitudes to Europe, and within European institutions it has gone some way to establishing Wales as a region capable of taking a leading role in Europe. Alongside the structures created by the European institutions and supported by the nation states, the regions have created their own groups which provide pressures on the central European institutions on behalf of the regions and give an opportunity for local representatives to share in the experience of other Europeans working in a common cause. Wales has been involved in this regional network through membership of the Conference of Peripheral and Maritime Regions (CPMR) and later through the Assembly of European Regions (AER).

CPMR was established in 1973 at the same time as the enlargement of the European Community from six to ten members, when Britain became a member. Wales was represented at the first meeting of CPMR in St. Malo by the Welsh Economic Council, although these representatives were not from an elected body. Wales was, however, present with 22 other regions who were also founder members of CPMR, and, after a gap in representation, the Welsh Counties Committee (later the Assembly of Welsh Counties) became members on behalf of Wales in 1982 and since then have regularly represented Wales at CPMR meetings.

The economic benefits of membership of the Community and the need to get the greatest benefit for their own region were the main reasons for membership of CPMR. The CPMR was an organisation established for and by the regions and the Welsh Counties Committee was able to make use of a consultant adviser employed by Clwyd County Council in gaining their early experience of what is now familiar international activity. While the main issues of concern at the CPMR were the economic development of the coastal and peripheral regions, the Conference increasingly saw the need for a further grouping that included all the regions of Europe and this enlargement became part of CPMR's objectives.

The CPMR also took up the themes of cultural identity of the regions. For example CPMR launched a network on cultural tourism in association with the Folk Study Centre (later called ECTARC) at Llangollen. Wales was given the responsibility for reporting on these issues as the CPMR cultural delegacy and, partly to provide a support for the CPMR, ECTARC was established at Llangollen by Clwyd with the support of the CPMR, the Welsh Counties and other bodies in Wales.

In 1985 CPMR members, with the Welsh representative, Councillor Elwyn Conway of Clwyd, playing a significant part, set up the Council of European Regions (later the Assembly of European Regions— AER). By 1990 there were 150 regions belonging to AER, including Baden-Württemberg with a population of nine million as well as some very small regions like Jura in Switzerland with a population of only 65,000. Wales was actively represented in the new AER and Councillor Ray Owen of Gwent became one of its Vice-Presidents. When the European Community appointed its Consultative Committee on Regional Development Policy, Councillor Owen became a member on behalf of the AER and Wales was again asked to follow the cultural brief and ECTARC became the secretariat for the AER group established to report on cultural matters.

The Welsh involvement in both the CPMR and AER helped to give recognition to an elected Welsh representation which was not appointed by central government and the Welsh delegations, for their part, helped in establishing the position of the regions in Europe, especially leading in the need for the protection and development of cultural diversity in Europe.

When the AER was established, the Union did not yet exist and the European Communities had not formally recognised either the regions or culture as being important for the development of Europe. Welsh representatives added to the pressure for such recognition and at its annual conference in Brussels in 1987, under AER president Edgar Faure, a former prime minister of France, a paper on the 'Cultural contribution of the Regions to the building of a united Europe' was given on behalf of the Welsh-led Cultural Affairs Group and was accepted as part of the AER programme for Europe as a single area. Both the recognition of the regions and the cultural role were later incorporated into the Maastricht Treaty—article 198 providing for the Committee of the Regions and article 128 for the support for national and regional diversity within a common European heritage.

Wales was able, through the AER and CPMR, to make its voice heard in Europe, making some contribution to policy and making contacts between elected representatives and officials. On a personal level Welsh representatives have been able to present Wales as a region to colleagues, especially through the work of the AER group concerned with culture. The Chairman of the Assembly of Welsh Counties (at the time Councillor William George, Gwynedd) gave the European delegates at an AER Cultural Affairs meeting in Cwmbran this verse which spoke through the Welsh language about the possibilities and hopes in Europe

Ewrob, y daw gobaith—o oes well	In Europe lies the hope of a better age
Wedi siom anfadwaith;	After prolonged enmities
Y ddaear dost, ddyddiau'r daith,	With wounded earth each day
Yn erfyn am hedd hirfaith.	Beseeching for long lasting peace.

ECTARC was established at Llangollen to support the cultural work of the regions in both CPMR and AER. It provides an independent base for regions in Europe concerned about traditional and regional cultures and is a venue for exhibitions with a regional association, a base for the promotion of exchanges of young people and a centre for conferences. Its direction comes from other regions in Europe as well as from Wales and is an example of Wales making a contribution to the regions of Europe.

Other groups of local authorities and other bodies in Europe are now forming and Wales is associated with some of them, such as the Atlantic Arc within the CPMR and the Bureau for Lesser Used Languages, with its base in Dublin but with a Welsh sub-committee. All are important for the shared experience of Wales as a region and, as another president of the AER, Signor Bernini said, 'the experience of those regions whose autonomy is more advanced should pull up regionalism as a whole.'

EXPERIENCE OF REGIONS OUTSIDE WALES

Those regions with constitutional structures that provide for sharing power between the centre and the regions, especially where the regional structure has helped in economic progress, have become models for those in Wales concerned with regional development. Baden Württemberg in Germany and Catalonia in Spain are both regions where economic success is perceived to be led by the region, and Wales has established good links with both of them. Interest in the Catalan experience has been increased because of historic Welsh sympathy with the region and the presence there of a significant minority language. There has been a readiness to learn from the Catalan economic and cultural revival brought about through the region's efforts.

After the Franco dictatorship came to an end in 1976 the new framework for democracy was, according to John Hooper in his *New Spaniards*, based upon the right 'of every region that wanted it to have access to a limited degree of autonomy' and the Spanish system established at the end of the 1970s became known as the '*estado de las automas*'. The new constitution also recognised within the regional structure the special position of the '*nacionialidades historicas*'—the historical nationalities which were identified as Catalonia as well as Galicia and the Basque country. These were given early recognition and powers, which were not necessarily the same as those given to other regions. The other regions were given a separate right to choose whether to become involved in the sharing of powers. The similarity between the concept of the historical nationalities and the nation region are such as to make the recent Catalan history of particular interest to Wales.

Catalonia was of personal interest, too, because its President, Senor G. Pujol has led a strong Catalonian delegation to AER and is now its president. He is President of Regional Government—the Generalitat—in Catalonia and the structure is such that the Government functions through a Parliament and Executive. The parliament has 135 members who are elected by proportional representation, and the system ensures that 'each zone of the Catalan territory has adequate representation'. (Catalan Parliament handbook) The parliament chooses the President and functions through committees to deal with legislation and control administration within the Regional Government. It has competence, both legislative and administrative, in language, education and culture and after a long period of prohibition by Franco, the Catalan language is actively supported by the Regional Government and is spoken by about half the population daily. The regional government also has competence in economic and public services within the region and restricted powers in fishing, mining and energy. It shares with the Madrid central government functions affecting the fiscal system. The main reservations to the central government of Spain are foreign trade and security, labour and business policy and social security.

With an economic growth rate of 5%, Catalonia has made good economic progress; it has become a centre for publishing in both Castilian and Catalan; it has built a reputation for style and design and showed in the staging of the Barcelona Olympics that it can provide a modern organisation that brings credit to the region.

Catalonia provides a good example of the European model of a real partnership between the state, the regions and the localities. If Wales receives devolved powers, it has a special opportunity to go on sharing the experience of regions like Catalonia and to build on it within Wales. The assembly of Welsh Counties (AWC) referred to the bilingual language skills being developed in Wales in their 1992 policy statement on Europe: 'Wales should identify its strengths, developing them to their full potential, not only in the economy but in other areas such as languages (building on bilingual teaching skills to include a third European language), the media, the peace tradition and music and sport.' The Catalan experience has shown that it is possible to combine determined support for culture and tradition with economic growth and, while Wales will need its own regional structure, there are important lessons that can be learnt from Catalonia and Spain.

COMBINED WELSH REGIONAL ACTIVITIES ON BEHALF OF WALES

Because of the absence of an elected Welsh Assembly, both the Secretary of State for Wales and the AWC have acted to represent

Wales as a region to other regions. Both had some basis for doing so—the Secretary of State, as political head of the Welsh Office (even though from central government), and the AWC (although from local government) as the next elected level of government below central government and both have been active in European work. Some of the recent Secretaries of State for Wales have lifted the level of European involvement by the Welsh Office and developed important protocols with some of the regions that had come to be familiar with Welsh contacts through the AWC.

The AWC has been replaced, following local government reorganisation, by a new Welsh Local Government Association which is currently determining its level of European involvement. During the period when the AWC participated as a regional body representing Wales, it became clear that it was a surprise to many regional representatives to find that a region should sometimes be represented by a central government minister who was not also an elected member of a regional assembly, and sometimes by elected members from the region who had no real regional powers. For the most part, however, the European regional representatives were pleased that a British region was ready to play a active part in Europe.

Co-operation between central and local government as representing Wales has been attempted even without adequate constitutional structures. There has been a determination to play a part in the new European structures and the link between the Welsh Office, through the Welsh Development Agency, and the local authorities in establishing a Welsh office in Brussels is an example of such co-operation. The WDA and the local authorities first established a representation of Welsh economic and other interests in Brussels through the private sector consultants, Coopers & Lybrand, but in 1991 a permanent Welsh office was established and supervised by a committee involving the participating bodies. The first assessment of its work finds that it has provided a valuable presence and can provide information on funds available for Wales, but it is not yet clear how much additional economic benefit this partnership has brought.

The Welsh local authorities, through the AWC, also made contact with Welsh MEPs on a joint basis and this led to a major conference and forum on Europe involving the MEPs in Cardiff in 1991, when AWC policy on Europe was presented. More recently the Europe

Forum set up in 1994 has brought together Welsh local authority representatives and members of the new Committee of the Regions. Whatever local authorities or the Welsh Office plan for Europe, and whether separately or together, it will not match in its present form the regional structures in other regions which there enable industry and commerce as well as social and cultural society to look to such a structure to make decisions within its own powers.

MINORITY RIGHTS

The growing European recognition of national communities which exist at a level below the nation state has given further support for the regions, especially those like Wales where the historic nation and region coincide. The protection of minority rights has become a way of acknowledging that such groups are vulnerable to assimilation by the majority and is 'a way of responding to nationalism in a larger state' in Hugh Miall's *Minority Rights in Europe*. The system in support of such minority rights is still being developed and is in need of urgent resolution—and a proper transnational structure.

Minority rights for groups within Europe have grown out of and alongside the protection of individual human rights, such as the right to life and liberty. These are themselves important in protecting the individual as a member of a minority in a national state.

Basic protection of these rights in Europe comes from the protection of the individual in the European Convention of Human Rights. First drawn up in 1950, and an important part of the work of the Council of Europe, the Convention protects individual right to life, liberty and security of the person, goes on to provide rights protecting the individual such as the right to freedom of thought, conscience and religion (article 9 of the Convention), the right to freedom of expression (article 10) and the freedom of association (article 11). The right to education according to the wishes of the parents has also been included in the Convention. As has been seen, the rights given by the Convention are regarded by the members of the Council of Europe as giving important and effective rights to individuals and are part of the working arrangements of Europe and their acceptance is generally made a pre-requirement of membership of the European institutions.

Minority groups are given direct protection through the rights given in the Council of Europe's Social Charter (1961) which gives support for minorities based on race, colour, language, religion, national origin, social origin, birth and other status by putting them on a footing of 'perfect equality' with other nationals within the state. The Charter has been seen as more a declaration of principles than a convention but remains a forum for consideration of the complaints of minorities, even if so far it is not a very effective one.

The Charter of Regional and Minority Languages of the Council of Europe seeks to give protection to people using minority languages in Europe. It was produced after some ten years of deliberation and compromise and provides minimum requirements to be placed upon nation states to promote languages traditionally spoken by nationals of the state who form a minority group and speak a language which is different from the language of the state. The Charter sets out a range of activities in public life, particularly in education, the courts and public administration and in the media and the arts which should be protected. The process is protected by a Committee of Experts who produce reports and to whom organisations can make a reference. It brings minority language groups to a formal body to which signatory members should respond.

The Charter was adopted in 1993 and as an international agreement still has to be signed by the states for it to apply in those states. Although the Welsh language may be better protected by central government in Britain than many other European minority languages, the Charter has not yet been signed by the British government.

There is the prospect of minority rights receiving further protection beyond that given by the Human Rights Convention, the Social Charter or the Charter of Minority and Regional Languages. The end of the Cold War and the resurgence of nationalism in Eastern Europe have pushed minority rights to the head of the European agenda and the protection of minority national rights has been seen as a way of avoiding nationalist claims for separation. It should provide a more acceptable solution, appropriate to a pluralist society, which is consistent with the European developments in the sharing of sovereignty referred to above.

In 1989 the Conference (now called Organisation) on Security and Co-operation in Europe (CSCE) adopted extensive minority provisions which included the right for the 'identity of national minorities to be protected' and for an expert committee to be provided with emergency powers of inspection. The Committee was given the power to publicise infringements and make recommendations, but had no direct method of enforcement. It was suggested by the Council of Europe that this could be incorporated in a new Charter for the Protection of Minorities.

The Parliamentary Assembly of the Council of Europe in 1993 also responded to the crisis in former Yugoslavia by proposing the guarantee of rights of national minorities by means of a form of legal protection similar to that given in the Human Rights Convention but extended to give rights of petition to groups as well as individuals.

These proposals were considered by the Heads of State meeting in Vienna in October 1993 and they seem to have linked both the alternatives. The Conference called both for a new framework Convention and an additional protocol to the Human Rights Convention. The new Convention would specify the principles of protection for minority nations and would be open for acceptance by non-members. The additional protocol for the Human Rights Convention would complement the existing Convention by guaranteeing further individual cultural rights, particularly for those belonging to national minorities. These proposals are still being considered but need to be available to provide stability in Europe. If the European institutions wait until a major conflict occurs between a nation state and the minority nations within it, it will be too late to handle a dispute effectively and another intergovernmental conference should consider a provision for the framework Convention and look again at the CSCE proposal for an investigating Committee.

The European protection of minority nation rights would have implications for countries like Scotland and Wales, particularly if the right of minority nations were to include some democratic right to an elected body to deal with issues like education and culture. It would supplement the benefits from a properly protected constitution and a national policy of devolution.

References and further reading.

E. Alfredson, *Equality and discrimination—minority rights*, Council of Europe.

Archer & Butler, *The European Community: Structure and Process*, 1992, Pinter.

M. Bassand, *Culture and Regions*, 1987, Council of Europe.

G. Carey, *On being European*, 1993, CAFE.

Church in Wales, *Wales in Europe. Core or Periphery,* 1992. Church in Wales.

Council of Europe, *Culture and Regions*, 1992.

Davie, Gill and Platten (Ed.) *Christian Values in Europe,* 1993 CAFE.

A. Drzemezeczewski, *European Human Rights in Domestic Law*, 1983, Oxford.

ECTARC, *Regional Diversity in Europe*, 1994.

European Commision, *Europe 2000*, 1991.

   Europe at the Service of Regional Development, 1994.

   Competitiveness and Cohesion:trends in the regions, 1994.

   Wales and the European Union, 1994.

T.C. Hartley, *Foundation of European Community Law*, 1988, Oxford.

Hogwood & Keeting, *Regional Government in England*, 1982, Clarendon.

S. Hooper, *The New Spaniards*, 1995, Penguin.

H. Miall, *Minority Rights*, 1994, Pinter.

J. Osmond, Ed. *A Parliament for Wales*, 1994, Gomer

J. Osmond, *Welsh Europeans*, 1995, Seren.

E. W. Wade, *Administrative Law,* 1988, Oxford.

   Law and Sovereignty, 1991, LQR I.

H. Woolf, *Protection of the Public*, 1989, Hamlyn Lectures.

Chapter 5

WALES: A NATION-REGION

As an historic nation Wales is able to play its part within the multinational state of Britain. It is one of the regions of the United Kingdom and as long as the separate historic culture is not maintained merely as a sort of 'family furniture' (Hobsbawm), the historic nation provides a proper basis for regional identity and pride. The development of Welsh political awareness has not generally been linked to the cause of separation from the Union and, following the 1997 General Election, devolution plans are again being presented on the basis of a proper status for the nation region within the UK and the European Union.

There have been various definitions of a region based upon economic, physical or historic patterns within a larger state but in the present context, the importance of the administration and government of the region is such that it is useful to define the region simply as that part of the state used for carrying out the devolved or decentralised functions of the central government. It is the political unit for carrying out government functions at the level which is above local government but below central government. The boundaries, in most cases, are fixed by administrative needs and are not necessarily identified with an historic area, let alone an historic nation. Whether or not there is a clear sense of identity as an historic nation, the region has become an important part of British government.

Apart from the administrative necessity of devolving government in a modern and complex state to the regions, the region can provide a constitutional safeguard against too much power being concentrated in one institution of government. The traditional division of governmental power is between legislature, executive and judiciary and is not always effective as a constitutional safeguard. Vesting some of the governmental powers in a region is an additional safeguard against excess power in the centre and is adopted in its clearest federal form by many of the Western democracies.

It provides an added sense of identity to have regional government carried out where there is a historic identity and the British regional structure in government has developed most within the historic nations of Wales, Scotland and Northern Ireland. This association of the nation and region gives credibility to proposals for Wales and Scotland to have a quicker rate of devolution and regional accountablity. In the case of Ireland, nationalism may have made independence inevitable in 1922 but it is likely that it was the failure to recognise the need for effective regional political structures that led to the separation of the Irish republic from Northern Ireland. In any case from 1922 the British regional consideration of Ireland has been related to that part still within the United Kingdom in Northern Ireland.

Within the member states of the European Union, the importance of the region as a governmental unit has grown at different speeds, but the regional unit has become a common administrative form, even though in Ireland the republic has chosen to make the whole country a European region. Britain has a clear regional structure for government but, unlike most European countries, has not yet a directly elected regional assembly to make such government accountable.

Within Wales the renewal of the sense of belonging to a historic nation has grown alongside the regionalisation of government and has become inseparable from it. The revival of Welsh identity coincided with the start of popular democracy and the growth of the responsible welfare state. From the ending of political control of Wales by the Tory landed gentry as a result of the Reform Act 1867, the main Welsh political aspirations have been in support of radical politics and not in a struggle for separation. They have led to campaigns for fair treatment for Wales and the recognition of Wales's special needs within the UK. These were the substance of early Welsh representation and early Welsh success led to several Acts of Parliament relating to key Welsh issues in education, land reform, church disestablishment and temperance. Some of the Welsh Liberal leaders, like T. E. Ellis and Lloyd George, also considered the imperial parliament in Westminster to be incapable of delivering adequately on many of these special Welsh issues and the case was argued for political and administrative devolution of government from Westminster. The result has been a century which has seen the establishment of Welsh institutions, calls for the decentralising of government departments to Wales, and proposals for direct accountability in Wales for some of the functions of government. The claims for more Welsh control over governmental matters have coincided with the need of central government to regionalise its activities and have eventually produced growing support for devolved government.

THE PERIOD OF LIBERAL NONCONFORMIST ASCENDANCY

TEMPERANCE, EDUCATION AND DISESTABLISHMENT AS WELSH ISSUES

The parliamentary aspirations of Wales until World War I were a political expression of Welsh nonconformity, as was discussed in a previous chapter. After the Reform Act of 1867 and until World War I, the Liberal Party dominated Welsh political life and the particular Welsh claims to government through the Liberal Party appeared in concern for education, disestablishment of the Church of England, land reform (including opposition to tithes) and a concern for Temperance and Sunday Observance. These issues were the Welsh political preoccupations of the time and many of the M.P.s were supporters of these Welsh causes first and party men second. Their motives were based upon the need for action for neglected Wales and according to K. O. Morgan they established 'a distinctly Welsh radical style in politics, less bitter and less strident than the nationalist movement in Ireland, but in its quiet fashion the more effective'.

The first Act of Parliament specifically for Wales in this new atmosphere was the Sunday Closing Act 1881 which protected the special nature of Sunday in Wales by closing public houses on a Sunday and at the time it was seen as 'a testimony to the identity of the nation' (K. O. Morgan).

Another successful Welsh Act of Parliament was the Welsh Intermediate Education Act 1889 which gave parliamentary success in the campaign for better education in Wales. Following national outrage at the condemnation of Welsh education and Welsh nonconformity by the education Commissioners in 1847 (the Treason of the Blue Books) the Welsh people had set about building an education system, which should be state provided and available to all children in Wales, whether Welsh-speaking or not. A committee, headed by Lord Aberdare, had reported to the government in 1881 that education in Wales should recognise the Welsh character, that the ban on speaking Welsh in schools which had been introduced after the 1847 Report should be withdrawn and that the Welsh language should be taught. It also recommended that, in addition to the national system of elementary schools introduced by the Education Act 1870, there should be a Welsh system of secondary and higher education. The committee's main recommendations were implemented and the 1889 Act gave the new counties in Wales the power to establish their own county secondary schools and to raise money through the precept on the rates for the purpose. By the mid-1890s county schools, later called County Grammar Schools, were provided in many Welsh towns by what were the first local education authorities in Britain. The Act also provided for the establishment of a system of inspection and examination in Wales through the Central Welsh Board, which was set up in 1896, and which became important in its own right as a Welsh institution.

The mood of Wales in support of education soon led to the provision of university education in Wales, first in Aberystwyth and then in Cardiff, Bangor and later in Swansea. In 1893 the Charter of the University of Wales was granted. The Welsh demands for a People's University were based on a desire to secure equality with the English and the ordinary people of Wales made their contribution to the establishment of the university so that their children should have the same educational privileges as their counterparts in England. The same national enthusiasm soon led to the establishment of the National Library of Wales in Aberystwyth and the National Museum of Wales in Cardiff, with both institutions receiving their charters in 1907.

Another single issue that made politics important for Welsh nonconformity at that time was the position of the Church of England as the established church in Wales. The majority of Welshmen were still Welsh-speaking and nonconformist and they deeply resented the claims of the Church of England. No Welsh-speaking bishop had been appointed between 1715 and 1870 and small tenant farmers, in particular, resented paying tithes to a church that was not theirs and was considered alien. It brought violent protest in rural areas and the nonconformists demanded change. A Tithes Act was passed in 1891: Gladstone said, in supporting the arguments, 'the nonconformists of Wales are the people of Wales'. A Disestablishment Bill was presented in 1891, in 1895 and again in 1909, but was strongly opposed by those within the Church of England and was only finally enacted in 1914 and then implemented after World War I. It brought about a separate disestablished Church in Wales and transferred the Church's non-eccesiastical charitable money to the county councils to hold as trustees for distribution within the counties. Although, as K. O. Morgan pointed out, it had ceased to be 'the central passion' of Welshmen by the time of its enactment, the disestablishment legislation was a major success in an area affecting fundamental Welsh attitudes to history and religion and represented the completion of the Welsh Liberal Nonconformist agenda.

DEMOCRATIC ACCOUNTABILITY

While popular support in Wales was directed to the issues associated with temperance, education and disestablishment, the new Welsh political establishment saw that there was also a need for separate Welsh institutions to match the new found political awareness. It led to the first attempts at devolution and the Liberal cause became linked to Home Rule, the appointment of a Secretary of State for Wales, and the establishment of government departmental offices in Wales

PARLIAMENT FOR WALES—HOME RULE

Home Rule, as the campaign for a separate parliament was known at the time, was not a popular cause in Wales in the nineteenth century. The Welsh had shown no sympathy with the Irish Home Rule campaign but Gladstone introduced the idea of a separate parliament for Wales to deal with all matters except for reserved issues like foreign affairs and central taxation. His slogan was 'Home Rule all round', with Scotland and Wales included in an attempt to make his plans for Ireland more acceptable. In 1887 Gladstone made an important speech in Swansea which presented the idea of Wales as a nation in the context of Europe and thousands are said then to have marched through the streets of the town in support of a Welsh parliament. T. E. Ellis worked with a newly created Welsh campaigning group, Cymru Fydd, to advocate a Welsh National legislature and an Executive to be jointly responsible to it and to the imperial parliament.

In 1890 Lloyd George declared for Home Rule with a plan that involved a general constitutional settlement in the form of 'quadrilateral home rule', which also included a separate parliament for England. He and others argued that Westminster would be better able to get on with its essential tasks if the home issues were shared with the devolved parliaments. This Home Rule was a general federal solution and not a plan for separation. A draft bill was introduced in 1912, but the Irish objected because they believed it would delay their own moves to devolution and the Bill was not then pursued. A Government of Wales Bill in 1914 provided for a Welsh parliament, an Executive and a Welsh division of the High Court, but the bill, prepared by the member for Denbigh, E.T. John, was defeated by the advent of World War I.

After the war Lloyd George, as Prime Minister, spoke about a European settlement that took account of the 'little five foot five countries' but although Home Rule received support from the House of Lords in 1919, the Irish crisis dominated home constitutional issues. Proposals for a parliament for Wales ceased to be on the main political agenda until well after the Second World War.

NATIONAL COUNCIL

Apart from the campaign for a parliament there were attempts at the turn of the century to establish a national advisory council based on the newly elected counties and county boroughs. In 1889 a proposal for a Welsh national body which would advise on matters of common interest in Wales was rejected and the Disestablishment Bill, 1895—providing for a national body to administer the non-ecclesiastical church funds of the Church of England in Wales—failed when the Bill was not proceeded with because the government went out of office before the royal assent could be given. Proposals for a Council of Wales to deal with education were made in 1902 and 1906 but agreement could not be reached by the authorities on the contributions to be made and these proposals also failed.

WELSH COMMITTEES IN PARLIAMENT AT WESTMINSTER

A proposal in 1888 to establish a Welsh standing committee of the House of Commons to deal with Bills in Westminster which related exclusively to Wales was opposed because special parliamentary procedures for Bills relating to a particular territory would be contrary to the unitary control of legislation by Westminster. This modest and sensible plan was consequently delayed until 1907, by which time the most active period in Welsh legislation was already over. It did, however, provide an acknowledgement of the need for special procedural provision in Westminster, even if, as happened nearly ninety years later over the Cardiff Barrage plans and Local Government reorganisation in Wales, the provision could be suspended if it did not suit the government.

THE OFFICE OF THE SECRETARY OF STATE FOR WALES AND A WELSH OFFICE.

Another campaign for the recognition of the special needs of Wales which started during the period of the Liberal ascendancy in Wales was that for the appointment of a government minister with responsibility to parliament for government action in Wales. Scotland had been provided with a Secretary for Scotland and a separate Scottish Office in 1885 and attempts were made to set up a similar ministerial post for Wales. As with other constitutional demands at the time, it was considered less important than obtaining legislation on specific Welsh needs. Proposals appeared in Bills before parliament on several occasions before 1914 but none of them obtained sufficient support and the argument was made that the office of Secretary of State for Wales would be an ineffective way of recognising Welsh needs. The main reason given foresaw some later difficulties. It was said that a Secretary for State appointed by a government which had only minority support in Wales could not claim to reflect the political views of Welsh people. Such was expected to be the case whenever there was a Conservative government.

While the case for direct ministerial oversight of Welsh affairs was not successful in the period before World War I, there was real success in securing separate government offices for Wales. This was based upon a need to deal with Welsh governmental matters by way of departmental decentralisation and pointed to the later establishment of the Welsh Office. A Welsh department was set up in the Board of

Education in 1907 and was attached to the Board in London with Owen M. Edwards as first chief inspector. As welfare provision by government was started, a Welsh Commissioner for Health Insurance was appointed in 1911 and an Agricultural Commissioner was appointed in 1919 in recognition of the importance of the needs of small and tenant farmers in Wales. Together the changes in government administration represent the early steps towards administrative devolution in Wales and were then seen as a more attractive alternative to the appointment of a Secretary of State. It was a response to Welsh national pressure rather than the need of central government departments to decentralise their activities into the region. Decentralisation was to become a feature of British government only during and after World War II.

Although the Liberal Party had supported devolution for Wales and had, at least after 1906, the parliamentary majority to legislate for it, the actual achievements had fallen short of this. They were, however, probably an adequate reflection of the expectations of the Welsh people—to make sure that some long held grievances were removed, to present Wales as a nation to be noticed and, because of the introduction of the popular vote, to take some limited constitutional measures to give effect to their sense of identity.

The Conservatives were unionist and opposed Welsh Home Rule and other claims for Welsh institutions of government as being divisive. They formulated their response to the urbanisation of the country and the grant of the popular vote with a renewed commitment to the intergrated union of the four nations. They responded to the new found power of an increasingly large electorate by municipalisation, and in particular, by using the new counties and county boroughs to provide local services. In Wales the Conservatives were ready to make use of the 13 counties and 4 County Boroughs established under the Local Government Act 1888 and specifically to empower them where there was need for extra provision in Wales, as in the Welsh Intermediate Education Act 1889. This emphasis upon local government was important and for a long time represented for many, including many who were not Tory, an effective and practical response to claims for separate national constitutional institutions.

THE INTER-WAR YEARS AND UNEMPLOYMENT

After World War I, the Liberal Party led by Lloyd George went into coalition with the Conservatives, adopted some of their policies and ceased to lead on the cause of devolution. The Liberal Party in Wales was split between those who remained loyal to Lloyd George and those who believed that the Welsh cause had been betrayed. At the same time, the Welsh-speaking nonconformist society that the Liberal Party had represented was in decline. Most of the people in Wales now lived in urbanised areas and the Labour Party became the main political voice of Wales. As was seen in Chapter 2, the Labour Party became the natural inheritors of the Liberal radical tradition and in 1922 won the largest number of Welsh parliamentary seats. They have done so ever since.

Kier Hardie had been MP for Merthyr from 1900 and had led the formation of the Independent Labour Party. He was a champion of democratic rights and his campaigns were based upon a socialist self-governing Wales rooted in the local culture. He supported the case for democracy, decentralisation and accountability, which fitted well with the radical tradition in Wales and in 1918 the Labour Party Conference accepted devolution as party policy and resolved in favour of statutory assemblies for Scotland, Wales and England.

The post-war period brought a major change of direction. The spectacular growth of the Welsh economy had come to an end; the failure of the coal markets and the slump that followed were disastrous. Wales was further damaged by the accepted economic policies of deflation and contraction and as a consequence Welsh unemployment reached 32% of the adult insured population; many left Wales and in the period 1921-1940: 430,000 left for work elsewhere. The Labour Party proposed centralist planning of the UK economy as the way to support the disadvantaged regions like Wales and by the mid-twenties any devolution proposals for Wales had been effectively dropped. Welsh influence in the Labour Party remained strong, however, and the radical political concerns in Wales were reflected in the Labour policies. Most important of these were the redistribution of wealth as a means of establishing a fair society and state planning of the main industries as the way out of misery and poverty. Survival through solidarity with others in the UK became a more relevant political cause than devolution.

Some Welsh intellectuals despaired of the new politics and were attracted by the cause of independence. Southern Ireland was considered by a few to be a political model and the Welsh Nationalist Party (Plaid Cymru) was formed in 1925. It argued that the other parties no longer offered support for the national symbols of 'land, religion and language'. The new party was seen then as a right wing party concerned with self government for the conservation of the language; it received no general support and provided no challenge to Labour.

The plight of the workers and the attraction of world communism made another new party more of a challenge to Labour in Wales than that of right wing nationalists. The Communist Party in South Wales was strong within the miners' union and, during the inter-war years, presented a Marxist, Soviet-style challenge to the new Labour ascendancy. They were most strongly organised in the Rhondda, but even here the communities at large remained loyal to the Labour Party.

While the economic and political upheavals of the inter-war years made devolution of government appear irrelevant, there was some general decentralisation of government administration. Decentralisation was an attempt by central government to resolve the conflict between the needs of central planning and effective control. It was not, however, based upon the recognition of Wales as a unit and, in some cases, worked against it. Departmental decentralising of the factory inspectorate, for example, separated Wales into north and south and for operational purposes placed the headquarters for the north in Liverpool and for the south in Bristol. It reflected the centralist view by emphasising the departmental need to decentralise and took no account of the historic region where the service was to be delivered.

The Conservatives were in government during most of the inter-war years and their policies, although different from the Labour Party, were also centralist and based on a unified UK. There was, therefore, no major party support for Welsh regionalism. It seemed to have disappeared with the failure of the Welsh economy and there was no change in attitudes until the Second World War and the planning for reconstruction thereafter.

DECENTRALISATION AND ADMINISTRATIVE DEVOLUTION (1945-1979)

World War II required a total civilian response to total war and, as part of government strategy, regions were established for each part of the United Kingdom. The object was to implement central policies of control of production and distribution in order to support the war effort. Scotland and Wales were treated as standard regions of central government, along with the regions of England, and this form of regional government has been maintained since then as a feature of the British Government. Although in England the standard region has not been adopted by each of the government departments as their regional unit, in Scotland and Wales the new regional boundaries of government departments coincided with the national boundaries.

Apart from the practical needs of governing in time of war, there was need to prepare for the peace that was to follow and the regions provided the basis for these plans. The Labour Party was included within the wartime coalition government, and, among some of their leaders, the need for economic action on a devolved basis to the regions became an important part of their plan for avoiding the disasters of the inter-war years. In Wales a separate Welsh Reconstruction Advisory Council was set up and Welsh regional structures were considered as a focus between local government and Government planning. The case for a specific regional response was led by the miners' leader, James Griffiths, who believed that the regionalisation of government offices should go further than the war plan. He called for a Welsh Planning Authority and led the Welsh Parliamentary Party in calling in 1943 for a Secretary of State for Wales.

The post-war Labour government made use of their experience of wartime regional arrangements and were ready to use regional solutions as part of their overall central plan. The regional solutions were, however, administrative and managerial and the nation's industrial and social revival took place under Labour's strong central government policies.

The supporters in the Labour Party of a political devolution were bitterly opposed by the party mainstream and this position was strongly maintained by Aneurin Bevan, a leading Welshman in the

111

party. He even opposed the introduction of distinct mechanisms in Westminster to consider separately Welsh matters and when the annual Welsh Day debate was introduced in 1944, he poured scorn on it, arguing that there were no issues which were exclusively Welsh which needed separate debate. The Labour view was that to avoid a return to inter-war conditions the goal should be an overall economic policy that could dispel mass unemployment in the depressed areas, including Wales. The state adopted economic planning, nationalisation and the establishment of the welfare state to give effect to this policy through the processes of central government. It allowed for decentralisation but not devolution and the decision-making rested firmly with government departments working through regional offices.

THE ESTABLISHMENT OF THE POST OF SECRETARY OF STATE FOR WALES

There was little support in the government for the Reconstruction Advisory Committee's proposal for a Secretary of State and a private members' bill in 1949 made no progress in parliament. It was the Conservative Party that took up the cause to the extent that as the opposition they submitted a plan for a Minister for Wales and in 1951 the new Conservative government gave effect to it with the appointment of the Home Secretary, Sir David Maxwell Fyfe, as Minister with responsibility for Welsh Affairs. The Conservatives had taken the initiative and developed it with further appointments during their period of government. The responsibility for Welsh Affairs was in 1957 placed with the Ministry of Housing and Local Government and a specific minister made responsible for Welsh Affairs. The Conservatives had taken the first steps towards the provision of regional political accountability.

The office of Secretary of State for Wales remained to be created and changes in Labour leadership and direction were to provide the opportunity. Aneurin Bevan, the champion of state planning, died in 1956 and with James Griffiths as deputy leader a proposal for the establishment of a Secretary of State post was included in the party manifesto in 1959. The Welsh Advisory Council view was that a Secretary of State should be appointed to exercise the powers of

Agriculture, Education, Health and Housing and Local Government in Wales and this was adopted.

The final step in the formation of the Welsh Office and the appointment of a Secretary of State came after Labour, led by Harold Wilson, was returned to power at Westminster in 1964. Harold Wilson recognised the post as necessary for 'the administrative convenience and greater recognition of the Welsh nation' and in October 1964 appointed James Griffiths as the Charter Secretary of State. James Grifffiths had maintained the Welsh case for separate recognition in the Labour Party and in Government and his appointment was 'a fitting finale to a long career which had seen his identification with his native Wales quite unshakeable', (K. O. Morgan). He was able to combine support for centralised planning with his belief in the political expression of Welsh identity and he saw his appointment as a means of providing a better way of conducting government business and of giving proper recognition to the Welsh nation.

The appointment of a Secretary of State was an important constitutional development for Wales as the office provides a democratic control of the Welsh government activities in Wales through the appointment of a territorial minister who is a member of the British Cabinet. He stands as political head of a government department and is accountable for its actions to Parliament and the Cabinet. The Secretary of State is responsible for integrating the functions of government in Wales into the one department and represents Welsh interests at Westminster.

The weakness of the appointment has been that the Secretary of State's accountability, both constitutional and political, is to the UK government, and this may not reflect political choice in Wales. It can result in the appointment of a Secretary of State who is not an MP from a Welsh constituency and this has been the case in the most recent appointments. It becomes difficult for the people of the region to accept the validity of such selection, particularly as, in some cases, the appointment has seemed to have more to do with achieving party objectives within the cabinet than with adequately providing accountability of government in Wales.

As a result of James Griffiths's determination the powers of government departments dealing with housing and local government, road transport and land planning were transferred to the new Welsh

Office. In 1974 a Permanent Secretary was appointed to head the civil service in the Welsh Office and gradually other Whitehall powers were transferred to it. By 1978 the powers of the Welsh Office were almost as extensive as those of the Scottish Office, and included Education, Industry and Agriculture.

When the finance grant was allocated for local government in a block system between England, Scotland and Wales, the formula for distribution known as the Barnett formula distributed financial resources on the basis of 85% to England, 10% to Scotland and 5% to Wales, and within the limit gave a wide choice of priorities to the Welsh Office. The policy direction remained, and still is, with the centre but the administration was firmly Cardiff-based. As a level of central government administration, the Welsh Office has generally been considered a success and an improvement in government. It has 'opened up a corner of government' (Kellas and Madgwick) to locally elected and other community leaders and brought better relations with local government because of the direct contact created.

PARLIAMENTARY RECOGNITION OF WALES

The appointment of a Secretary of State and the setting up of the Welsh Office were practical recognition of the separate historic position of Wales. So too was the further allocation of time for Welsh affairs in parliament itself. It was a process that evolved slowly—a Welsh Day had been introduced in 1943 but had not been taken seriously by many Welsh MPs. A request for a Welsh Grand Committee was refused by Labour and it was a Conservative move in 1960 that granted this debating opportunity to Welsh MPs four times a year. Later Welsh question time in Parliament was established once every three weeks during Parliamentary sessions and, after the General Election in 1979, a Welsh Select Committee was appointed to give more detailed consideration to particular Welsh issues.

WELSH NATIONAL COUNCILS

More significant than such parliamentary recognition was the development during this period of government-sponsored national councils for Wales. One demand that had existed earlier in the century had been for a national council to deal with education matters in Wales. The priority given to education had continued throughout the century but it was not until 1948 that the Welsh Joint Education Committee was established. This body built on the work of the Central Welsh Board and, as with a number of other bodies established after World War II, was local authority based and related mainly to their functions, many of them carried out jointly on a Welsh basis. The Welsh Joint Education Committee was, however, constituted by statutory order and was important as a supplement to central government in providing a regional role in education in Wales.

More related to central government in Wales was the development of nominated advisory bodies to represent the views and needs of Wales to central government. In 1949 one response to a Parliament for Wales Campaign had been the establishment of such an advisory council. James Griffiths had argued successfully in the Cabinet for this response and was able to obtain agreement that the Council should advise on cultural and economic matters affecting Wales. He was not able to get agreement to the appointment of a ministerial chairman for the council but a leading Welsh trade union representative, Huw T. Edwards, was appointed as Chairman and he was a strong supporter of devolution and saw the advisory council as a first step to a parliament for Wales. When a report from the Council recommending the appointment of a Secretary of State and the creation of the Welsh Office was rejected he resigned.

The Advisory Council carried on until 1966 and then became a part of the 1964-70 government process for regional planning in all regions. Economic planning boards were established throughout the UK and in 1968 a new all Wales Advisory Council under Professor Brinley Thomas took over the functions in Wales and continued until 1979.

While the Advisory Council represented part of the changing political scene in Wales, it had no executive powers and functioned as a governmental body, although ready to give independent advice. Similarly, the Welsh Development Agency which was formed in 1976 and the Development Board for Rural Wales which replaced the Development Corporation for Mid Wales in 1977 were governmental bodies appointed and accountable to the Secretary of State. They did, however, represent a further and important extension of government in

Wales. With the Welsh Office and the Welsh Advisory Council, they were practical moves to devolution without direct accountability to the Welsh electorate.

STEPS TOWARDS AN ASSEMBLY

The post-war movement for an elected body for regional government in Wales was even more tentative. For the three decades between the end of the two world wars, there had been little concern in Wales about an elected assembly or parliament. There was a revived call in 1949 with the establishment of a Parliament for Wales Campaign, based on the need for a directly democratic form of devolution. The old arguments appeared pressing the case for a parliament which would exercise some of the powers of central government in Wales. The names of the parliament campaigned for have varied—'council', 'senate' and 'assembly', but the objective has always been an elected body to represent the nation-region of Wales. Nearly all of them have been proposals for a new form of intermediate government between central government and local government.

The first post-war campaign was an all-party organisation. One of the leaders was Megan Lloyd George, the daughter of the former Prime Minister, but Labour MPs like Goronwy Roberts who were also campaign leaders, were ridiculed in Westminster. The Deputy Prime Minister, Herbert Morrison, was opposed to any devolution as, of course, was Aneurin Bevan and there was no general backing among Labour Welsh MPs. In 1955 a petition in Parliament received the support of only five Labour MPs. The campaign also had little Labour support in Wales where it was still considered irrelevant to the needs of the country.

The renewed official Labour support for political devolution did not happen until after the appointment of the first Secretary of State for Wales and then, more than fifty years after the Labour Conference had resolved in favour of devolution, the Welsh Labour Conference proposed an 'elected council' for Wales. Their plan did not include any legislative powers but proposed again the creation of a representative body for the country. It was followed by an official working party reporting to the Secretary of State for Wales, by then another noted supporter of devolution, Cledwyn Hughes who was

116

appointed in 1966. He put the working party proposal for an elected council to the Cabinet but other cabinet ministers, including the Secretary of State for Scotland, blocked the proposal because they feared the result would have been a similar plan for Scotland, (K. O. Morgan). In Scotland the Conservative opposition leader, Edward Heath, at Perth in 1968 proposed establishing a Scottish Assembly and in his speech he referred to the need for power to be spread as widely as possible throughout the community, but this was not pursued by the Conservatives when they came back into government.

Wales's third Secretary of State was George Thomas who was committed to Wales in speech and action but a determined anti-nationalist. He reflected a strong view in the Labour Party that was unable to support a Welsh Assembly because it seemed a step towards separatism. The moves for an elected body were met by the establishment of the 1968 Advisory Council for Wales and with the appointment in 1969 of a Royal Commission on the constitution of the UK, chaired by Lord Crowther and then, after his death, by Lord Kilbrandon.

The Commission was not limited to consideration of the constitutional position in Scotland and Wales but this became its prime concern. It took four years before the Commission reported and then it was split into several different views. There was, however, a large majority recommendation for a legislative assembly for Scotland and an elected council for Wales with executive powers—a large minority (six out of thirteen) recommended a senate for Wales with legislative powers. Although the report was not precise enough to satisfy any particular group, the majority view of the Commission suited the mood of the Labour Party policy of Harold Wilson 'to democratise and decentralise'. The return of the 1974 Labour government gave him the opportunity to take further parliamentary action.

THE 1979 REFERENDUM

When Labour returned to office in 1974 they set about implementing their policy of democratising and decentralising government institutions, including proposals for devolution in Scotland and Wales. Devolution has been described as the transfer of powers from

Parliament to a subordinate body on a geographic basis, (Bogdanor). It did not create a federal system because there was not a division of powers within the state under a constitutional settlement and it was in this setting that a White Paper in 1974 set out principles of legislative devolution in Scotland and executive devolution in Wales. Two further White Papers—in 1975 and 1976—sought to provide more detail, such as the relation between the office of Secretary of State, which was to be retained, and the elected body. A Bill was produced in 1976 but opposition among Labour MPs led to the provision of a clause for a referendum and even then, the Bill failed on a procedural step. There was opposition from MPs to the introduction of the clause for a referendum in an already published bill and a guillotine motion to make progress was defeated, and the whole bill failed. In 1977 provision for legislation was put in two bills proposing devolution separately for Scotland and Wales and they received Royal Assent in 1978.

The Wales Act seemed both complicated and unrelated to the particular needs of Wales and many Labour members of Parliament who had been prepared to vote the Bill through spoke against the proposal in the referendum. Among the opponents was Neil Kinnock, Labour MP for Bedwellty and a future leader of the Labour Party. He maintained a campaign against the Bill and devolution but as leader of the Labour Party some fifteen years later shared in the fundamental change within the Labour Party, and led his party into the 1992 election with a proposal for a Welsh elected body.

Although the devolution of Welsh Office powers and duties to an elected body under the Bill would have meant the regional devolution of central government, Labour Party councillors and others in the newly (1973) strengthened and enlarged counties in Wales saw the Assembly proposals as a threat to the new pattern of local government established only five years previously. While the new assembly would not be local government, the divide between central and local functions seemed blurred and, especially as the previous Labour proposals in 1965 were for a Welsh elected council which took over local government functions, there was widespread support for the opposition to the Referendum.

Entry of the UK into the European Community and the elections for the European Parliament provided another argument, namely that the

Assembly would add yet another new tier to elected government. It was said that it would result in too much democracy with elections for councils or parliament at five different levels—community council—district—county—Westminster and Europe and that was considered unacceptable.

The Referendum held on 1st March 1979 had few supporters. The proposals may have been illogical but, as Vernon Bogdanor points out, this illogicality of the constitutional proposals could have been overcome if there had been the political support. This was not forthcoming. Apart from the party opposition of the Conservatives and a significant part of the Labour Party in Wales, the proposals did not appeal to major groupings in Wales—the Welsh-speaking Fro Gymraeg feared domination of the Assembly by south Wales socialists, and the Valleys and Marcher Wales feared control by Welsh speaking nationalists and a drift to separatism. The referendum massively rejected the proposals—only 11.8% of the total electorate voted for an Assembly and, in actual votes, it received only 20% of the votes cast overall and was rejected in each of the eight counties.

It appeared that the idea of a separate elected assembly for Wales had come to an end. George Thomas could write 'the whole business of a Parliament for Wales is now dead.' The Conservative success in the General Election that followed in May brought Mrs Thatcher into power and in Wales the Conservatives, who had opposed devolution, had their best result of the century, winning eleven seats and 32% of the votes, as if to confirm the opposition of Wales to an Assembly.

THE NEW CENTRALISM

THE GROWTH OF THE WELSH OFFICE

The new 1979 Government led by Margaret Thatcher was committed to the market economy and control of inflation, even if it involved increased unemployment, public expenditure cuts and a growth in central control. In Wales, Conservative support at the election had risen to 32% of the vote as a result of one of the largest swings to the Conservatives in the UK. It put them in a stronger position in Wales than at any time during the century and the combined effect of the Referendum on Devolution and the General Election result seemed to endorse Westminster as the sole legitimate source of important political decisions. Historian Gwyn A. Williams thought Wales had 'finally disappeared into Britain'.

The Referendum and the proposals before it had, however, shown what was politically possible and, as in the 1950s, it was the initiatives of the Conservative government that created the atmosphere for a further review of the constitutional needs of Wales. In the period after 1979, the consequence of government policy in Wales was to strengthen the Welsh Office. It maintained its role as a small goverment department which carried out its civil service functions and, with government policies, presented the Welsh case for a proper share of resources. The economic policies of the government brought restructuring of industry accompanied by massive unemployment in Wales and the Welsh Office was given additional powers. Some of these powers were transferred from local government and many were exercised by agencies appointed and accountable to the Secretary of State and the Welsh Office (the Welsh 'quangos'). With the Conservative minority position in Wales, political control of government in Wales became an important issue and led to revived interest in the case for an assembly.

The representation of Wales in Europe was another regional role claimed by the Welsh Office. Although Wales had been among the least enthusiastic supporters of the European Community in 1976, reliance upon European Regional policy by the government for grants for economic renewal in the disadvantaged regions made for greater awareness of the benefits of membership. The Welsh Office was concerned to become an effective part of the European regional network and, as has been seen, a Welsh Office section dealing with European matters was established, followed in 1990 with WDA led representation at Brussels. Overseas representation in the European Union was necessary to achieve the best results for Wales as a region and gave new significance to the territorial responsibility of the Welsh Office; it also brought Welsh representation alongside that from other regions in Europe where there was a proper democratic basis for the government.

The Welsh Office grew during the 1980s and the early 1990s as a regional centre for the exercise of central powers and became more obviously an intermediate level of government. Many of the services provided by the local quangos might have been provided by local authorities but the exercise of authority through the Welsh Office made these activities constitutionally part of central government. Its powers have increased to include Welsh Higher Education and it provides the departmental framework for nearly all the home department functions of government, except for those of the Home Office. The use of appointed bodies by central government is not new, but since 1979 there has been an increase, especially at local level, in the number of quangos—it is estimated by John Osmond that in Wales in 1997 there are more quango appointees than elected councillors.

The reduction in the role of local government has been general in the UK but in Wales and Scotland government changes have brought about the total removal of one of the government levels; in Wales the eight large counties were abolished by the Local Government (Wales) Act 1994 and replaced by a larger number of unitary authorities. Whatever may have been the merits of the move, the Government has by taking out one layer of representation reduced the 1979 argument that an Assembly would bring an extra level of government to Wales.

Since 1979, there has also been an extension in the range of powers of quangos—in 1993/4 the revenue budget of Welsh quangos was £2.4 billion: 34% of Welsh Office expenditure, (Osmond). The growth in the power of the Welsh Office and the use of unelected quangos has been a major part of the case of the Labour Party for an elected Assembly.

CONSULTATIVE COMMITTEES

One of the positive features of the Welsh Office intermediate role in Government has been the extension of the consultative process between central and local government in Wales. The system was backed by the officials of both the Welsh Office and local government who jointly provided the research and working papers for the consultative committees in formal session. The main consultative body was that on Local Government Finance, with regular meetings held between the Secretary of State and elected representatives of local government—the Welsh Counties Committee and the Council of Welsh Districts. While the total amount of money available for grant distribution was decided by central government, the working framework for assessing relative needs and distribution was the result of careful and shared professional consideration. The process enabled the deliberations, if not the decisions, to be shared and made for a small area of non-confrontational government at the Welsh level. A similar committee was set up for higher education in Wales and this, too, held regular and joint meetings between elected representatives from the local education authorities and the minister in the Welsh Office concerned with education. Similarly there was a body for consultation between the housing authorities and the Welsh Office. The value of the consultation process diminished as the Wales Advisory Body on education was wound up and housing became less of a local government function and from 1991 there was a preoccupation with the government plan to reorganise local government into unitary authorities. The process, at its best, was, according to J. Barry Jones, one of the successes of the new administrative devolution and brought more credit to the Welsh Office than similar procedures in England.

PARLIAMENTARY COMMITTEE ON WELSH AFFAIRS

The administrative devolution to the Welsh Office might have been mirrored by parliamentary control by MPs. When the parliamentary select committee system was applied to the Welsh Office in 1979 it was seen by some as a possible alternative to devolution. Its duty was to act as a parliamentary watchdog over the affairs of the Welsh Office by providing a non-partisan invigilator of the Executive and was intended to become an influential lobby for Wales. The Select Committee had as its immediate audience Parliament and the Government, particularly the Welsh Office civil servants, but it also addressed organised interests and public opinion in Wales and for some time it looked as though it might become a substitute for the Welsh Assembly. It was, however, limited in its functioning because it had to work within the rules applying to a committee of the House of Commons. It had little authority to act independently of the parliamentary reporting system which assumed that MPs had a duty to act for their constituency and for the country but not for their region. The parliamentary procedure made it difficult to provide sub-committees to carry out some of the necessary investigative work and it did not employ the range of staff needed for an effective audit so that much of the most critical work was done by the Audit Office serving the Public Accounts Committee and the Welsh Committee itself tended to pursue broader policy matters. After the 1983 General Election, the standing of the Select Committee was reduced because the government was unable to provide the required government majority in membership of the committee from their back bench Conservative members in Wales and they had to bring in MPs from outside Wales. The Westminster parliamentary system was seen 'not able to work satisfactorily in Wales because of the scarcity of Conservative MPs' (J. Barry Jones) and because rules could not be adapted to suit the territorial purpose.

Apart from the experiments in regional structures with the Welsh Select Committee, Welsh MPs were able to rely on the parliamentary processes previously established—the eight days for parliamentary questions, one Welsh day debate and four sittings of the Grand committee to raise matters affecting Wales and the Welsh Office. The former Welsh Secretary, William Hague, said the government was prepared to strengthen the Welsh Grand Committee by increasing the number of meetings, some of which would be held in Wales.

The potential for the development of the Welsh Grand Committee is similar to that which was seen for the Welsh Select Committee but as an argument against an assembly, it is unlikely to succeed because it functions within the Westminster parliamentary procedure. The limited value of such provisions as a constitutional protection was shown in 1994 in government action on the Local Government (Wales) Bill, when the government suspended Standing Order 86, which allows all Welsh MPs to participate in the committee stage of specifically Welsh legislation. With only six conservative MPs for the 38 Welsh constituencies, the government would have been unable to obtain a majority on a vote and, faced with that, the Welsh safeguard introduced in 1907 was suspended (John Osmond). The Welsh Grand Committee is generally a party occasion and does not have adequate mechanisms to provide oversight of the elaborate patterns of government in Wales for which the Secretary of State is responsible. If the Welsh Select Committee failed to provide the mechanism for such accountability, question time and Grand Committee debates cannot be expected to do so.

Efforts to establish an effective regional mechanism for accountability for the Welsh Office and its quangos through the Westminster process have failed and the government has recently returned to the concept of a nominated advisory body, (John Osmond). In March 1994 a Welsh Economic Council was established by the Welsh Office 'to ensure greater cohesion and a more united effort on the part of the Principality's major employers' and employees' organisations'. The Council might have helped to express Welsh views on economic and social matters but its nominated and private nature made it very unlikely that it would meet the demands for a representative body for Wales.

PARTY PLANS AND THE FUTURE

The administrative devolution of central government to the Welsh region has been a major element in the recreation of Wales as a nation. The Conservative position in Wales has been to oppose an assembly but its own policy has revived pressure in Wales for an Assembly. The growth of the Welsh Office, the diminution of local government, the development of government by quangos, the cutbacks in public spending, the increased dependence on European regional policy, and the government of the UK by a party with minority backing in Wales all made a plan for an Assembly a common policy of the other political parties in Wales.

The Labour Party no longer believes in a centrally planned economy and the long period in opposition has renewed arguments for democratic accountability in Wales so that Labour MPs from areas traditionally opposed to devolution have become the leaders in the campaign for an Assembly. The Labour Party consultation on devolution and its paper 'Shaping the Vision' showed their limited expectations for an elected assembly. It, and the subsequent policy documents, are directed to the main issue of the accountability of the Welsh Office and the quango bodies. Constitutionally a referendum would give additional status to any subsequent bill and provide an implicit protection against later repeal of the devolution without another referendum. The form of representation to an assembly remains contentious within the Labour Party but the case for proportional representation has received cautious approval. This may yet result in a system which would reflect more nearly the overall voting pattern in Wales and combine it with a firm basis of local constituency representation.

The Liberal Democrats and Plaid Cymru both support devolution for Wales—the Liberal Democrats argue for a federal constitutional settlement which includes an assembly in Wales with legislative and tax-raising powers: Plaid Cymru would go further and, putting the emphasis upon small sufficient communities, seeks a position in Europe that is separate from England and the English regions. Both will want, if possible, to support the Labour plan as a move in the right direction.

There is support for an Assembly from a non-party 'Parliament for Wales' Campaign which, through a committee chaired by Dewi Watkin Powell prepared in 1966 a report with proposals for legislation. At the same time Dr John Marek, the Labour MP for Wrexham introduced a Bill into Parliament entitled the Government for Wales Bill and this, too, is seen as a means of enabling a more detailed debate to take place on what form devolution should take.

At the time of the 1997 General Election, the Conservative Party was the only mainstream party in Wales to oppose a regionally elected body. It believed that political accountability can be met by representations in the British Cabinet and that an elected assembly would represent a threat to the union of the United Kingdom. It is worth remembering, however, that there has in the past been Conservative support for devolution, such as that given by Edward Heath in 1968 and by Lord Hailsham in 1976. In addition, many of the most significant steps in establishing the regional importance of Wales have come from Conservative governments, including the ministerial overseeing of Welsh Affairs in 1951, the establishment of the Welsh Grand Committee in 1960 and the Welsh Select Committee in 1979.

The history of any country provides a framework within which each generation may draw its own understanding of its past and its prospects. In Wales it seems that in the sixteenth century the country's leaders firmly attached the country to England and, with the Tudor monarchs, helped to create the nation-state which is still today the

United Kingdom. In the first half of the present century the majority of the urban working class in Wales identified themselves and their country with the other workers within the UK and they led in forming the British Labour movement. As the twenty-first century approaches, an opportunity arises for political and constitutional renewal from the British and European review of sovereignty, the nation state and centralist government. The result of the General Election in 1997 transformed the British political situation, with a new goverment elected on a platform of constitutional reform. In the United Kingdom and Europe there is an expectation that there will be accountable regional government in Scotland and Wales and within this setting, Welsh identity and experience could enable the people of Wales to benefit from its development as a nation region and play a leading part in a new constitutional pattern of effectiveness and accountability.

References and further reading.

V. Bogdanor, *Devolution*, 1979, OUP.

E. Chappell, *Wake Up Wales*, 1943.

R. Coupland, *Welsh and Scottish Nationalism*, 1954, Collins.

The Constitution Unit, *An Assembly for Wales*, 1996,. UCL.

E. J. Hobsbawm, *Nations and Nationalism since 1780*, Cambridge, 1990.

Hogwood and Keating, *Regional Government in England*, Clarendon, 1982.

Geraint H. Jenkins, *People's University*, 1994, WEA.

J. Barry Jones, 'The Welsh Office—a political expedient or administrative innovation', 1990, *Cymmrodorian Trans.*

J. G. Jones, 'Early Campaigns to secure a Secretary of State', 1988, *Cymmrodorion Trans.*

J. G. Jones, 'Socialism, Devolution and a Secretary of State', 1989, *Cymmrodorion Trans.*

Jones & Wilford, *Parliament and Territoriality*, 1986, University of Wales.

Kellas & Madgwick, *Territorial Dimension in UK politics*, 1982, Macmillan.

K. O. Morgan, *Labour People*, 1992, Oxford

K. O. Morgan, *Wales: Rebirth of a Nation*, 1981, University of Wales.

J. Osmond, *The Democratic Challenge*, 1992, Gomer.

J. Osmond, Ed., *A Parliament for Wales*, 1994, Gomer.

Gwyn A. Williams, *When was Wales?*, 1985, Penguin.

APPENDIX

Names of counties and county boroughs established under Section I and Schedule I of the Local Government (Wales) Act 1994.

Counties.

Anglesey/Sir Fôn.
Caernarfonshire and Merionethshire/Sir Gaernarfon a Meirionydd.
Cardiff/Caerdydd.
Cardiganshire/Sir Aberteifi
Carmarthenshire/Sir Gaerfyrddin.
Denbighshire/Sir Ddinbych.
Flintshire/Sir y Fflint.
Monmouthshire/Sir Fynwy.
Pembrokeshire/Sir Benfro.
Powys/Powys.
Swansea/Abertawe.

County Boroughs.

Aberconwy and Colwyn/Aberconwy a Cholwyn.
Blaenau Gwent/Blaenau Gwent.
Bridgend/Pen-y-bont ar Ogwr,
Caerphilly/Caerffili.
Merthyr Tydfil/Merthyr Tudful.
Neath and Port Talbot/Castell-nedd a Phort Talbot.
Newport/Casnewydd.
Rhondda, Cynon, Taff/Rhondda, Cynon, Tâf.
Torfaen/Tor-faen.
The Vale of Glamorgan/Bro Morgannwg.
Wrexham/Wrecsam.